"Gene Veith was one of the fi ...gage postmodernism over twenty years ago. Now he teams up with Pastor Trevor Sutton to use Lutheran theology—particularly the chief article of justification by faith alone—to provide readers with a robust and thoughtful apologetic. I was especially pleased with the authors' use of the work of the counter-Enlightenment thinker Johann Georg Hamann in articulating a response to Postmodernism. Theological themes of Christology, biblical interpretation, Law and Gospel, vocation, sanctification, and the two kingdoms are aptly covered. This book will spark conversations and fuel a more confident Christian witness in our day."

—Rev. John T. Pless
Assistant Professor of Pastoral Ministry & Missions;
Director of Field Education,
Concordia Theological Seminary, Fort Wayne, IN

"This book shows that we now live in a post-secular world where anti-Christian attitudes have no privileged stance for setting the agenda for public discourse. It is high time that Lutherans roll up their sleeves, and like Paul in Athens share the Gospel in the *agora* of ideas. Veith and Sutton demonstrate that unlike Puritan, Revivalist, or Roman Catholic views of Christian faith, Lutherans are well positioned to share God's Good News to a world fragmented by modernity and postmodernity."

—Dr. Mark Mattes
Chair, Department of Philosophy and Theology,
Grand View University, Des Moines, IA

"I'm convinced that the best way to understand another tradition is to listen to its most articulate, informed, and passionate advocates. This book certainly fits that bill for those who want to understand Lutheranism. You don't have to agree with everything (I don't!) to appreciate the rich delights that Luther and his spiritual heirs bring to the feast."

—Dr. Michael Horton
J. Gresham Machen Professor of Systematic Theology and Apologetics,
Westminster Seminary California; co-host of the White Horse Inn,
and author of Core Christianity

"This scintillating study, which combines the literary and cultural expertise of Veith with the historical and theological wisdom of Sutton, shows how classical Lutheranism addresses the concerns of the postmodern world in a surprising way. It is daring in its claim that Lutheran theology does full justice to the paradoxes of God's revelation and human life, provocative in its conviction that Lutheran practice unites what is separated in other denominations, and enlightening in its clear exposition and apt use of fresh illustrations."

—*Dr. John W. Kleinig, professor emeritus at the Australian Lutheran College (formerly Luther Seminary) in the University of Divinity, Adelaide, Australia*

"Half a millennium after Luther's Reformation, Protestantism seems hopelessly in decline. God has been banished from objective reality. The Gnostic heresy denying the significance of the body is experiencing a resurgence, to wit feminist theology. Yet, in this astonishing book, Gene Veith and Trevor Sutton boldly and brilliantly argue that in the next 500 years an authentic church will survive, but as a Metachurch, a church beyond the church, and it will have a distinctly Lutheran flavor stressing God's Word, His nearness, His presence in the Sacraments and every Christian's priesthood rooted in the divine purpose found in his everyday work."

—*Dr. Uwe Siemon-Netto, Director Emeritus, The League of Faithful Masks, Capistrano Beach, CA*

"The Holy Christian Church has always had both its resident Deceivers and Truth Tellers, or those skilled at promoting the doctrines of man versus the doctrines of God. Regardless of motivation, the end result is always defense and support of either heterodoxy or orthodoxy. To countervail heterodoxy, idolatry, and heresy, God the Holy Trinity has unfailingly raised up Christian *Parrhesiasts* who witness yet once again to the Holy Scriptures as the final authority on matters of doctrine. Dr. Veith is one of those Truth Tellers. I cannot recommend highly enough his new book *Authentic Christianity*; he and Pastor Sutton skillfully sort out the pillars of truth from the pillars of falsehood. This monograph is consistently engaging from cover to cover."

—*George V. Strieter, Publisher, Ballast Press*™

"Veith and Sutton partner to bring forward a rich in detailed history, systematically sound, and a complete practical approach to our Lutheran theology as applied to the world yesterday, today, and tomorrow. *Authentic Christianity* is informative, thought provoking, and easily accessible. For those wondering how our Lutheran Confessions compare to other denominations, this is the resource for you. It will be the go-to reference material for Christians to fully understand how we are to live out our vocations as faithful Christ followers. *Authentic Christianity* comes at just the right time, the 500th Anniversary for the Reformation. What better time to clarify and confess our faith? Kudos to Veith and Sutton, job well done at just the right time."

—*Rev. Eric Ekong, Senior Pastor,*
Trinity Lutheran Ministries, Jackson, MI

"Culture has changed; Lutheran theology has not. As a result, Lutheran theology must not be adjusted to keep up with the times but be reintroduced to individuals, people who are often tossed around by the waves of every cultural ideology. And that is just what Veith and Sutton have done in this marvelous book. Whether you are a spiritual nomad looking for truth or a lifelong Lutheran, this book speaks Lutheran theology—Authentic Christianity—to people with postmodern ears and individuals learning to navigate within this new culture. This excellent book is a superb tool for recovering the Authentic Christianity of the past while embracing and applying it to whatever lies before us."

—*Rev. Dr. Matthew Richard, Zion Lutheran Church, Gwinner, ND;*
Author of Will the Real Jesus Please Stand Up? 12 False Christs

"Veith and Sutton show that Christianity is not a product of human experience but founded on God's revelation. Addressing the contemporary forms of Christianity that have failed to reach the rising tides of postmoderns, the authors contend for an authentic Lutheranism that can make sense of people's suffering and give lives meaning for today and eternity. The answer is not yet another 'style' of Christianity. Instead, Veith and Sutton boldly call for a 'new' Reformation that is a continuation of Lutheranism's first principles: God's justifying Word, life-giving Sacraments, and the purpose of the individual's divine callings."

—*Rev. Christopher S. Esget, LCMS Sixth Vice-President*
Senior Pastor, Immanuel Ev.-Lutheran Church, Alexandria, VA

"Engaging, in the truest and freshest sense of that word; that's what Veith and Sutton provide for us here. First, while many thinkers neatly engage textbook worldviews that are difficult to find in real life, this book tackles the messy fluidity of this world's 'prettified gods.' Second, while many Christians nowadays propose withdrawal from the world as the best option for dealing with evil, these authors contrastingly assert that faith is realized and fulfilment is found as we engage virtuously within the arenas of real life. Finally, conscientious readers will embrace the Holy Spirit's lure in this book to engage personally in enduring questions such as: 'Why am I really here?' 'What is real freedom for?' and 'Who is my neighbor?'"

—*Rev. Dr. John Arthur Nunes,*
President, Concordia College New York

"This book is a refreshing, re-presentation of the full power of the Lutheran proclamation of the Gospel for the sake of the Church and the world in which we all live. For the layperson, the pastor, the scholar, or the seeker, if you are looking for a book that roots and strengthens your faith as well as one that demonstrates the power of the life of faith lived out in the world of today, then this book is for you!"

—*Dr. Gregory P. Seltz,*
Executive Director, the Lutheran Center for Religious Liberty
Speaker of The Lutheran Hour, Emeritus

Gene Edward Veith Jr. and A. Trevor Sutton

AUTHENTIC CHRISTIANITY

How Lutheran Theology Speaks to a Postmodern World

CONCORDIA PUBLISHING HOUSE • SAINT LOUIS

TABLE OF CONTENTS

ABOUT THE COVER

Edvard Munch is the Norwegian artist best known for *The Scream*, a painting acclaimed for capturing the modern and postmodern condition. But Munch, for all of his rebellion and mental illness, had grown up in a devoutly Lutheran family. Here, in *Golgotha*, as some bystanders look away while others are drawn into the cross, Munch brings Christ into the world of *The Scream*.

PREFACE

Brian McLaren, a central figure in the Emerging Church Movement, wrote a book some years ago called *A Generous Orthodoxy*. It had a significant subtitle: *Why I Am a Missional, Evangelical, Post/Protestant, Liberal/Conservative, Mystical/Poetic, Biblical, Charismatic/Contemplative, Fundamentalist/Calvinist, Anabaptist/Anglican, Methodist, Catholic, Green, Incarnational, Depressed-Yet-Hopeful, Emergent, Unfinished Christian* (Zondervan, 2004). McLaren hoped to get beyond these divisions and dichotomies in favor of a more relational Christianity that transcends all of these traditions. But something is curiously missing from McLaren's title and chapter headings: Lutheran. In the list of traditions he wants to draw from and identify with (sort of), he mentions Evangelical, Catholic, Methodist, Calvinist, Anglican, and Methodist. But Lutheran does not appear.

Authentic Christianity argues that the Lutheran tradition does what McClaren is hoping for. The Lutheran tradition offers a framework for pulling together what is best in all other Christian traditions. And it embodies an expression of Christianity that can uniquely address the postmodern condition that McClaren is hoping to reach. But the Lutheran tradition does so not by being "emergent," or making up some new approach to church or to the Christian life. Rather, it does so in an unexpected way: by being confessional, sacramental, and vocational.

This book is a collaboration between an aging academic and a young pastor. The former has been on a pilgrimage from liberal Protestantism, through "mere Christianity," through 1960s-era syncretism, to evangelicalism—including a flirtation with Calvinism, and at last to Lutheranism. The latter is a millennial raised on Lutheran theology, pastoring a congregation, and attending a secular university. Coming from two very different places—different generations, different vocations, different entries into Lutheranism—the authors have unique perspectives on how Lutheran theology engages contemporary life.

Gene took the long road to Lutheranism. In his studies of postmodernism, the history of ideas, literature and the arts, and the relationship between Christianity and culture, he has found Lutheran Christianity to be a reliable guide through the labyrinths of life.

As an infant, Trevor was baptized in a Lutheran congregation. He went to a Lutheran church as a child. He went to a Lutheran university and seminary. He did everything but grow up in Lake Wobegon. This has resulted in some good, but nagging, questions that Trevor has engaged throughout his life: Are you Lutheran only because you were raised Lutheran? Could it be that Calvinism, Catholicism, Orthodoxy, or the Emergent Church offer a better articulation of the faith? What does Lutheran theology offer that cannot be found elsewhere?

These questions have been answered. Sensing that any other vocation would not be entirely satisfying, Trevor attended seminary and entered into the pastoral ministry. Though he has not been a pastor for very long (five years), he has personal experience in how Lutheran theology engages contemporary culture. He has seen troubled souls find peace when he spoke words of absolution—"In the stead and by the command of my Lord Jesus Christ I forgive you all your sins . . ."—to an individual tired of waiting for an inner feeling of Christ's forgiveness. He has used simple tap water in the hospital to deliver the eternal promises of Holy Baptism to people longing for the presence of God in the midst of suffering. He has distributed the body and blood of Jesus to people craving the nearness of God. He has watched mixed-up millennials find eternal purpose in their vocations. In addition to being a pastor serving in a congregation, Trevor is also a graduate student at a large research university teeming with postmodernists, secularists, and those who are "spiritual but not religious." His personal experience confirms that Lutheran theology can and does speak to disaffected evangelicals, disillusioned secularists, and burned-out believers. The topics discussed in this book are not mere speculation; they are borne out in personal experience.

This book is about how Lutheran spirituality can inform contemporary Christianity in a way that addresses the spiritual struggles today. We believe Lutheran Christianity offers a sort of "metachurch" that contains and comprehends the best of all Christian traditions, while also having a life of its own. And, just as it sparked a Reformation of the Church five hundred years ago, Lutheran Christianity can do the same today.

We want to thank several people for helping make this book a reality. We would like to thank Laura Lane and the rest of the team at Concordia Publishing House for their help with this project. Gene would like to thank his wife, Jackquelyn, who agreed to take time out of their busy retirement for him to write this book. He would also like to thank Tonny Sørensen of Denmark, who brought Gene over to Scandinavia in an effort to help bring back Lutheranism into those secular lands. Gene's thinking and lecturing over there about how that might be done played an important part in the genesis of this book. Trevor would like to thank his wife, Elizabeth, and daughters, Grace and Hannah, for their unending support and encouragement. He would like to thank his colleagues in the Writing, Rhetoric, and American Cultures department at Michigan State University for challenging him intellectually and welcoming a Lutheran preacher into their midst. And, finally, Trevor would like to thank Gene for his willingness to work on a collaborative project with a young pastor and writer.

To God be the glory!

PROLOGUE: A DIFFERENT WAY OF BEING POSTMODERN

The thesis of this book is that Lutheran Christianity is particularly equipped to address the postmodern condition. As such, Lutheran theology, spirituality, and practice have the potential of connecting with contemporary culture and reaching the secularists of the twenty-first century.

But this claim is ridiculous at face value. For, postmodernists are relativists who believe that truth is a personal or a cultural construction. They are subjectivists. Lutherans, on the other hand, are rigorously objective. They have so many doctrines, all of which they hold to be true. They believe in such things as objective justification and the objective presence of Christ in the objectively physical bread and wine of Holy Communion. And Lutherans are so churchy, with their congregations and their Church Year and their liturgical worship. They are a far cry from the free-wheeling, anti-institutional, spiritual-but-not-religious syncretism that characterizes postmodernist religion. If anything, Lutheranism would seem to be the opposite of postmodernism. But there are different ways of being postmodern.[1]

If anything, Lutheranism would seem to be the opposite of postmodernism.

---

1   For the account of modernity and postmodernity that follows, see the book by one of the present authors, Gene Edward Veith, *Postmodern Times: A Christian Guide to Contemporary Thought and Culture* (Wheaton, IL: Crossway Books, 1994).

PREMODERN, MODERN, POSTMODERN

The modern era began, says Thomas Oden, on July 14, 1789, with the fall of the Bastille.[2] The French Revolution overthrew the old order and replaced it with a new regime ostensibly based on reason and reason alone. The members of the monarchy were guillotined, ancient traditions were erased, and a new calendar based on a metric system purged the old Christian holidays and started history over again, with the proclamation of the Republic counting as the start of Year One. In Notre Dame Cathedral, the stained glass windows, crosses, and other works of religious art were smashed. A ceremony that involved crowning a woman dressed in classical garb was held, thus rededicating the cathedral and the nation to the Goddess of Reason.

That gesture defined the modern era. Reason would reign. And it would be invested with religious faith and devotion. The eighteenth century would become known as the Enlightenment, the so-called Age of Reason. To be sure, there were conservative rationalists, as well as the revolutionary rationalists. And there were still traditionalists and advocates of the "premodern" way of thinking. But there was a pervasive sense that all of nature and all of life could be fully understood and controlled by the autonomous human mind. The problem with Christianity, according to Enlightenment standards, was its supernaturalism and its dependence on revelation and miracles. Some theologians tried to eliminate those "nonrational" elements from Christianity, turning it into a this-worldly code of individual and social improvement. Others sought to replace Christianity with

---

2   Thomas Oden, *Two Worlds: Notes on the Death of Modernity in America and Russia* (Downers Grove, IL: InterVarsity Press, 1992), 32. See also Oden's *After Modernity . . . What? Agenda for Theology* (Grand Rapids, MI: Zondervan, 1990), which argues that postmodernity makes possible a recovery of orthodox Christianity.

the "rational religion" of Deism, which features a deity who imposes his rational mind on his creation, thus accounting for the rational order that can be found everywhere. But this rational deity does not interfere with the ordered system he set into motion; he leaves human beings to their own autonomy.

The nineteenth century became even more modern, as the analytical reason of the Enlightenment was complemented with the empirical rationalism of the scientific revolution. The Enlightenment brought about the belief that a god was necessary to account for creation, though he was superfluous after that. With Charles Darwin (1809–82), creation could be explained solely in terms of natural processes, so a god was not necessary at all. By applying the economic laws of the socially transforming industrial revolution—survival of the fittest and improvement by competition—to nature, Darwinism also promoted belief in progress. Human beings were getting better and better.

Such "modern" ideas accelerated in the twentieth century. Progressive educational theories assumed that teaching children could be reduced to a science like chemistry, initiating the new generations into modern life. Progressive politics took different forms and developed different ideologies—populism, socialism, social democracy, communism, and more—but they all had in common the assumption that a utopian social order could be established based on a rational philosophy, the implementation of a rational plan, and the application of human expertise.

It wasn't long before every area of life had been subject to modernization. This meant throwing out the past—its traditions, discoveries, and achievements—and starting all over again, based on new principles. Thus, among other things, society created modern art, modern poetry, modern architecture, modern design—and, most important, modern theology, which not only promoted a scientific approach to the Bible, explaining away its supernatural elements, but also recast Christianity according to a variety of "modern" ideas: psychotherapy, existentialism, Marxism, and the like.

But for all of the convictions of progress, all of the trust in what autonomous human beings could accomplish if they only threw off the shackles of the past, the modern age of the twentieth century was far from utopian. The century began with World War I, which was closely followed by World War II, which was, in turn, followed by the Cold War, including hot outbreaks throughout the world, such as the Vietnam War. Modernist ideologies that sought to solve society's problems by means of experts and central control became totalitarian monoliths. In the name of progressive ideas, modernists erected concentration camps and committed genocide. Modern technology indeed made life easier, but it also gave us poisonous gas, long-range bombers, and nuclear weapons. The modern economy saw an increase in wealth and raised standards of living, but it failed to eliminate poverty, turned creative workers into tenders of machines, and, ultimately, promoted materialism and greed.

Oden says the modern era ended on November 9, 1989, with the fall of the Berlin Wall.[3] At the time, Marxism was a supreme modernist ideology, offering a rationalistic explanation for *everything* in terms of economics, class struggle, and its all-encompassing philosophical system. But its real-world application in Communist Russia proved horrific, causing the death of millions, the establishment of a police state, and thought-control on a massive scale. By 1989, few citizens of the Soviet Union or its far-flung empire believed in Communism anymore. Then the entire Soviet system, despite its military power and its secret police, collapsed. The populations, young and old, rose up; soldiers refused to fire on their compatriots;

---

3   Oden, *Two Worlds*, 32.

government *apparatchiks* walked out of their offices to join the protesters in the streets. In Berlin, residents from both sides of the divided city tore down the wall that separated them. The wall that had become the emblem of Communist oppression—and the ideology it represented—had fallen.

So the modernist era lasted exactly two hundred years, according to Oden's signposts, from the fall of the Bastille in 1789 to the fall of the Berlin Wall in 1989. That is, from the victory of the first radically anti-traditional revolution, which was determined to remake society completely on the basis of reason alone, to the failure and implosion of a similar revolutionary project. What happened with Communism should not have been a surprise, for something similar happened at the very beginning of the French Revolution: the exhilaration of "Liberty! Equality! Fraternity!" turned into the Reign of Terror and the tyranny of Napoleon. (In contrast, as scholars have pointed out, the American Revolution was essentially conservative in its retention of Christianity, English law, and the tenets of classical republicanism. Nevertheless, America would become a quintessentially "modern" nation.)

Oden's period of exactly two hundred years might seem a little too neat, with an ending a little too late. Charles Jencks suggests modernism ended and postmodernism began at exactly 3:32 p.m. on July 15, 1972, with another act of demolition: the razing by explosives of the Pruitt-Igoe housing project in St. Louis, Missouri.[4] Built in the confidence of the 1950s, the multiple square blocks of featureless high-rises were designed to fight poverty by solving the housing problems of the poor. Instead, almost immediately, they became centers of crime, drug-addiction, and hopelessness. Since the residents didn't own the buildings, the structures quickly fell

---

4   Charles Jencks, *The Language of Post-Modern Architecture* (London: Rizzoli, 1984), 9.

into neglect and disrepair. Far from ending the problems of poverty, this urban housing project made them worse. Finally, government officials decided to give up on the whole idea, and the Pruitt-Igoe buildings were blown up, brought down by explosive charges and reduced to rubble.

But that emblematic demolition job, like that of the Berlin Wall, rested on prior disillusions. Already the general public had noticed the way modern urban renewal projects tore down beautiful old buildings and destroyed neighborhood communities, replacing them with ugly, impersonal boxes of concrete and steel, and building freeways to disperse the population into the suburbs. The artifacts of modernity began to seem soulless, shallow, and life-draining.

"Postmodern," as an alternative to "modern," had its origins in the 1960s. The reaction against the Vietnam War and technocratic society crystallized in the "counter culture" and found a home on university campuses. Objective rationalism gave way to subjective irrationalism, the product of "mind-expanding" drugs, psychological quests, and the sexual revolution. The Civil Rights Movement for African Americans was replicated with liberation movements for other minorities, women, and gays. This contributed to the rise of group identities, rather than the autonomous individual identities cultivated by modernists. A new awareness of various cultures, prompted by a rise in immigration and American diversity, manifested itself in multiculturalism and then cultural relativism. Burgeoning technology affected society in new ways. The manufacturing of tangible objects in the American economy gave way to the making and consuming of information. Personal computers, the internet, smartphones, and video games gave us virtual reality—as well as virtual identities, virtual social networks, and virtual relationships—contributing to the sense that all truths are imaginative constructions. Pop culture, the entertainment industry, music, television, and many other cultural factors contributed to the transition from the "modern"—with its rationalism, its idealism, and its seriousness—to something more open, more experiential, and more multi-faceted, a new cultural mood known as "postmodernism."

As all of this was happening in the culture, new thinkers and scholars were subjecting "modern" thought to a withering critique. Modernists projected a detached observer rationally analyzing objective reality so as to achieve absolute certainty. These new scholars exposed that model as an illusion. The observer is not detached but biased and culturally conditioned. Certainty can never be achieved. Truth claims are not discoveries but *constructions*. The same is true of moral principles, political ideologies, and religious convictions.

The French critic Jacques Derrida deconstructed not only the defining texts of modern and Western culture but also language itself. Because, as he said, "There is no transcendent logos," there can be no such thing as objective meaning, whether in a work of literature, a collection of laws, or speech itself. Michel Foucault showed that not only texts but also great ideas and time-honored institutions are "masks" designed both to express but also to hide the power relationships in a culture, thereby keeping the oppressor in control.

In the academic world, such thinking can be found in and sometimes also dominates nearly every field—literature, history, philosophy, law, the social sciences, education, theology—with the exception of science and mathematics, still bulwarks of modernism. This critique of objectivity and reduction of culture to power politics is the source of the "political correctness" that has paralyzed intellectual life on so many college campuses.

Thomas Oden considers this postmodern*ism* to be nothing more than "hypermodernism."[5] The modernists used their reason to be

---

5   Oden, *Two Worlds*, 79.

skeptical about everything. Then they turned their skepticism on reason itself. At any rate, this kind of thinking would seem to be at a dead end. If there is no truth, how can anything be studied? If there is no right and wrong, only impositions of power, how can there be politically-correct moral indignation? If the postmodernists are correct, all that can be done is to seize power for oneself or one's own group and oppress one's opponents in turn, using language to keep the public in line. If truth and morality are relative, there would seem to be no way forward.

Given these dead ends, some people are saying that postmodernism is over. The destruction of the World Trade Center on 9/11 might be a good marker for that. The airliners crashing into the buildings would be examples of realities that were not mere constructions, and the cruelty of Islamic terrorism would cast doubt on the postmodernist notions that all cultures, all moral systems, and all religions are equally valid. For, a little while after that catastrophe, America did seem to set postmodernism aside—invoking absolutes like good and evil rather than relativistic bromides—but then postmoderism reasserted itself with a vengeance. The new lesson from 9/11 is that all cultures, moral systems, and religions are equally invalid. And people who insist on holding to absolutes are equivalent to terrorists.

Oden says that if modernity, along with the hypermodernity of the postmodernists, has failed, the way to be actually postmodern is to contemporize the premodern. That is, to explore premodern ways of thinking and to bring them, where possible, into contemporary life. That does not mean replicating premodern ways of life, as in doing away with our technology or returning to the feudal system. Each age has its particular blindspots, shortcomings, and evils. Rather, Oden is recommending that we learn from the past and apply its insights into our present life. That includes, specifically, rediscovering historic orthodox Christianity.[6]

Indeed, whereas the modernists insisted that everything be "new," to the point of eliminating decorative touches in architecture and old-fashioned styles in the other arts, postmodern taste is quite open to the past. Postmodern architecture borrows elements from earlier styles—the classical, the gothic, the Victorian—and works them into contemporary-looking buildings. Today's films are often renditions of earlier times. Urban planners trying to cultivate a sense of community, which has been a casualty of modernism, look to older examples—such as the village where people lived, worked, and played in close proximity and city neighborhoods before the advent of the automobile. Contemporary environmentalists, locavores, and localists are rediscovering the land and cultivating a sense of place as their ancestors knew it. Oden recommends that we do the same—drawing on the past to address contemporary problems—when it comes to religion. And Lutheranism, which had its origins in the Renaissance transition between the old and the new, can show us how this can be done.

THE RATIONALISTS, THE NIHILISTS, AND THE LUTHERANS

There were counter-Enlightenment voices as far back as the Enlightenment itself. In the nineteenth century, the Romantic Movement—with its exaltation of emotion over reason, of the beauties of nature over understanding it analytically—was dominant for a while. And the nineteenth-century critics of the Enlightenment and the early twentieth-century critics of modernism are the forebears

---

6   See Oden, *After Modernity.*

of today's postmodernist thinkers. Derrida's deconstruction of language rests on the existentialism of Martin Heidegger and earlier existentialists, who taught that because there is no objective meaning in life, we must create meaning for ourselves. Similarly, Foucault's reduction of ideologies and institutions to their power relationships rests on Friedrich Nietzsche's notion of the will to power and to his philosophical nihilism.

Although we speak of periods such as the Enlightenment or Modernity as if everyone at the time followed their tenets, the anti-modernists, with their cultivated irrationalism and subjectivism, exercised great influence of their own. For example, the Fascists of the 1930s and 1940s were modernist in seeking to rebuild society from the ground up, but their Nietzschean view of power, their tribalism, their constructivist view of morality, and their neo-pagan rejection of the West's biblical heritage (which they branded as "Jewish") derived from the irrationalists and the existentialists, and, indeed, could be described as postmodernist.[7]

But another early critic of the Enlightenment, perhaps the most penetrating of them all, was neither an irrationalist nor a nihilist, but a devout, confessional Lutheran. Johann Georg Hamann (1730–88), though largely forgotten until his recent rediscovery, was a prominent figure during his lifetime. The poet Johann Wolfgang von Goethe considered him "the brightest mind of his day." Hegel hailed his "penetrating genius." Kierkegaard ranked him with Socrates and called him one of the "most brilliant minds of all time" and the "greatest humorist in Christendom."[8] Another fan was C. F. W. Walther, one of the founders of The Lutheran Church—Missouri Synod, who often quoted Hamann in his writings.

---

7   See Gene Edward Veith Jr., *Modern Fascism: Liquidating the Judeo-Christian Worldview* (St. Louis: Concordia, 1993).

8   John Betz, *After Enlightenment: The Post-Secular Vision of J. G. Hamann* (Chichester, UK: Wiley-Blackwell, 2012), 2–3, 14.

Hamann was a young member of the German Enlightenment crowd, eager to cast off the shackles of the past in the name of reason and reason alone. In London on a failed business trip, Hamann found himself penniless and despondent. On a whim, he started to read the Bible. He was overwhelmed. The Law and the Gospel did their work. He began to understand that the Word of God was addressing him personally. He read the account of Cain's murder of Abel and realized that "I, too, am Cain." "I could no longer hide from God that I was the murderer of my brother, that I was the murderer of his only begotten Son." But then he read about the blood of the brother crying from the ground (see Genesis 4:10). No sooner do "we hear the blood of the redeemer crying out in our heart than we feel that its ground has already been sprinkled," he wrote, "that the same avenging blood cries grace to us." As he read God's Word, he felt the Holy Spirit taking him deeper and deeper into faith in Christ. "The Spirit of God continued, in spite of my great weakness, in spite of the long resistance that I had previously mounted against his witness and his stirrings, to reveal to me more and more the mystery of divine love and the benefit of faith in our merciful and only Savior."[9]

Hamann's conversion was all-consuming. His Enlightenment friends, including his Königsberg neighbor Immanuel Kant, were alarmed at the change in him and worried about his new religious convictions. They met with him to try to argue him out of his unreasonable beliefs. Hamann's response—preserved in correspondence and developed into a series of books on a wide variety of topics, written in a uniquely witty and enigmatic style—was to demolish the most basic assumptions of the Enlightenment.

"Faith is no work of reason and therefore cannot succumb to any attack by it; for *faith* arises as little from reasons as *tasting* and *seeing*

---

9   Quoted in Betz, *After Enlightenment*, "The London Writings," 31–32.

do."[10] You yourselves, he said in effect to his rationalistic friends, hold many beliefs to which reason could not lead you. And reason can lead to conclusions you don't necessarily believe. Hamann took apart the Enlightenment model of the disinterested, serenely detached individual subjecting the world to completely objective judgments. Such objectivity is impossible, he showed, because it overlooks the very human biases, preconceptions, and prior beliefs that no one can escape.

Rationalistic thinkers were proposing elaborate systems that purported to explain virtually everything. Hamann argued that none of those systems, for all of their supposed basis in rational analysis, would even last. "The system of today, which provides the proof of your presuppositions, will be the fairytale of tomorrow."[11] Here he has been prophetic. Think of the succession of thinkers in the history of philosophy, each of whom constructs a logical metaphysics, which is then superseded by the next philosopher and a new logical metaphysics. Think of the all-encompassing but now discredited "metanarratives" of Hegel, Freud, Marx, and the various utopian ideologies. Consider what that record suggests about the all-explaining systems still taken seriously today, such as Darwinism and even the various schools of postmodernism.

Hamann also probed the rationalists' insistence on absolute certainty. Unless you can prove a proposition beyond any shadow of a doubt, using logic and scientific evidence, says the rationalist, I will not believe it. René Descartes experimented with radical skepticism, systematically doubting everything that could be questioned in an effort to find unquestionable truth, which, for him, was "I think; therefore, I am." He could be certain only of his own existence.

---

10   Quoted in Betz, *After Enlightenment*, 83.

11   Quoted in Betz, *After Enlightenment*, "The Magi of the East," 96.

Although Descartes would build on that foundation, finding reasons to believe in the existence of the outside world and even of God, he demonstrates how the quest for complete certainty leads, ironically, to complete doubt, leaving the self alone, knowing nothing, and isolated from reality. In showing how the obsession with rational certainty makes objective reality dissolve completely, leading to utter nihilism, Hamann goes beyond critiquing modernism. He is anticipating and then critiquing what would come: the postmodernists.

Hamann does that even more with perhaps his most influential contribution to the history of ideas: the role of language in human thought. There can be no philosophy, no ideas, no thought apart from language. Moreover, as he said, "Reason is language."[12] Attempts to arrive at absolutely certain conclusions based on reason alone, apart from all traditions and cultural biases, are futile, because the language used to formulate those conclusions is charged with tradition and culture. Hamann developed this insight in his "*Metacritique*" of Kant's philosophy and applied it throughout his later writings.

Thus, Hamann may well have been responsible for the "linguistic turn" in twentieth-century philosophy. This emphasis has taken different forms. The movement known as "linguistic analysis" examines age-old philosophical concepts and shows them to be "nothing but language." Such so-called analytic philosophers are mostly logical positivists, convinced—in a modernist way—that the physical world is all there is. Postmodernists also stress the role of language in thought. They often employ Nietzsche's metaphor of "the prison house of language." That is, since our very thoughts are conditioned by the words we use, all of which are culturally determined, we cannot escape our language. Jacques Derrida purports to show that

---

12   Quoted in Betz, *After Enlightenment*, 130, from a letter to J. G. Herder.

since there is no "transcendent logos," language itself lacks objective meaning. Trapped in the prison house of language, we can never go beyond it, so that we can never fully know any kind of objective truth. This is a primary basis for postmodernist relativism. Different cultures have different languages and each represents a different construction of reality. But since language itself offers only an illusion of meaning, there is actually no meaning anywhere, and we are left with nihilism.

But for Hamann, there *is* a "transcendent logos": the *logos* of the first chapter of John:

> In the beginning was the Word, and the Word was with God, and the Word was God. He was in the beginning with God. All things were made through Him, and without Him was not any thing made that was made. In Him was life, and the life was the light of men. . . .

> The true light, which gives light to everyone, was coming into the world. He was in the world, and the world was made through Him, yet the world did not know Him. He came to His own, and His own people did not receive Him. But to all who did receive Him, who believed in His name, He gave the right to become children of God, who were born, not of blood nor of the will of the flesh nor of the will of man, but of God.

> And the Word became flesh and dwelt among us, and we have seen His glory, glory as of the only Son from the Father, full of grace and truth. (vv. 1–4, 9–14)

God's Word—the *logos*—underlies all things. The whole creation came into being "through" God's language. God's Word—the Bible—is conveyed by means of human language, which thus *does* have meaning. God's Word comes to us not as reason but as *revelation*.

Christianity is not one of those systems or ideologies or "metanarratives" that fails because *Christianity is not a construction of human reason but a revelation of God Himself.* Reason itself is possible only by God's *logos*, the word from which *logic* is derived. Reason, however, can never be "alone," for it, too, requires *faith*—first, faith that the external world has an order and a meaning that reason can discern; then, faith in a mind behind the world that gives it intelligibility, thus, faith in God and, ultimately, faith in Jesus Christ, the Word made flesh. Language may be a prison house for those who reject God's Word, the autonomous selves who deny truths they cannot understand. But God's Word can break into the prison house and bring liberation to the captives by conveying Christ, who humbled Himself to the point of dying on the physical cross for their objective justification. Enlightenment, for Hamann, comes not from rejecting tradition in the name of reason, but from knowing "the true light, which gives light to everyone" (John 1:9).

Hamann wrote about not only philosophy, but also history, linguistics, politics, and aesthetics. He sought to "see all things through Christ."[13] Writing also in the field of theology, Hamann marveled at the *kenosis* of God, how He empties Himself of His majesty to descend to human beings in all of their limitations and sins: God the Father's creation and providential care for all that He has made; God the Son's incarnation and death on a cross to atone for the sins of the world; God the Holy Spirit's presence in the ordinary words of Holy Scripture. Betz summarizes what he calls "Hamann's most fundamental point" saying this:

> The *transcendent* God is kenotically hidden *within* language—just as he is kenotically hidden within creation, just as he is kenotically hidden within human history, just

---

13   Betz, *After Enlightenment*, 133.

as he is kenotically hidden within the humanity of Christ, and just as the Holy Spirit is kenotically hidden within the "rags" of Scripture. In sum, on the basis of this vision of the kenosis of transcendence, which is able to find the *transcendent* God *in* this world under the various guises of his love, Hamann points the way to a theological recovery of nature, history, language, and art.[14]

The modernists attempted to reduce nature, history, language, and art to simple rationalistic principles. The postmodernists lost them altogether. But Hamann's Christian perspective, Betz thinks, can bring them back by rediscovering their basis in the Father, Son, and Holy Spirit.

Betz believes that Hamann offered the best critique of the Enlightenment and thus, by extension, of Modernism. He also anticipated many of the ideas of today's postmodernists, while at the same time offering an alternative to them. Betz believes that Hamann should be mentioned with the reigning "postmodern triumvirate" of Nietzsche, Heidegger, and Derrida. The difference is that those three lead to the dead end of nihilism. Hamann, though, offers a way forward. The only choice we have, according to Betz, is between Hamann (that is, the Christian faith) and nihilism:

> Anticipating the collapse of secular reason, Hamann thus brings us to a decidedly postmodern crossroads, at which point one can take the road of faith, which, as an inspired tradition attests, leads to ever greater enlightenment; or one can take the road of postmodern unbelief, which leads to nihilism. Simply put, the alternative is one between Hamann and postmodernity.[15]

---

14   Betz, *After Enlightenment*, 340.

15   Betz, *After Enlightenment*, 319.

Betz elsewhere describes the Hamann alternative as "post-secular."[16]

POSTMODERNITY AND ORDINARY LUTHERANISM

Although Hamann has been called the most sophisticated critic of the Enlightenment,[17] his teachings amount to little more than ordinary Lutheranism, as we will discuss later in this book: the limits of human reason and the necessity of God's Word; the centrality of faith; the distinction between Law and Gospel; God being approachable solely through His incarnation in Christ; the theology of the cross versus the theology of glory; God revealing Himself by means of His physical creation in Word and Sacrament; God's hidden presence in the secular realm.

Hamann's critique of Enlightenment rationalism differs little from Luther's critique of Christian rationalism. Medieval scholasticism had turned Christianity into a system of logical syllogisms—as we see in the *Summa* of St. Thomas Aquinas—grounded in Aristotelian philosophy. This resulted, Luther believed, in a distant God whose grace and forgiveness were obscured by moralism, institutional power, and a world-denying piety. Luther's remedy was the same as Hamann's: the limits of human reason and the necessity of God's Word; the centrality of faith; the distinction between Law and Gospel; God being approachable solely through His incarnation in Christ; the theology of the cross versus the theology of glory; God revealing Himself by means of His physical creation in Word and Sacrament; God's hidden presence in the secular realm.

To be sure, Hamann's "post-secular" alternative to nihilism is the

---

16 Betz, *After Enlightenment*, 312, 337–40.

17 See http://www.iep.utm.edu/hamann/.

Christian faith. That faith manifests itself in many theological traditions, all of which are alternatives to nihilism. But Hamann drew on distinctively *Lutheran* teachings—such as the kenoticism of Luther's theology of the cross, the sacramental quality of Scripture, and even the complex nuances of Lutheran Christology[18]—to counter both the Enlightenment skeptics and the post-Enlightenment nihilists. These distinctively Lutheran teachings should have a special resonance for modernists and postmodernists.

Modernism and postmodernism are more than abstract philosophies. Most modernists and postmodernists probably have never heard of the key figures of these movements. Most have probably never heard of the terms *modernism* and *postmodernism*. Modernity and postmodernity are *conditions*. They are attitudes, frames of mind, and assumptions. That is, they are worldviews.

Contemporary culture consists largely of people who believe truth is relative, that they can choose their own morality, that life has no particular meaning. There are still modernists who believe that the material world is all there is and that the only reality is what science can prove. They have declined in number, but the new atheists have perhaps given them a boost. We still hear the argument from uncertainty, those who insist that they cannot believe in the existence of God unless it can be proven beyond the shadow of a doubt. The postmodernists, on the other hand, are "spiritual but not religious." They believe all religions are equally valid and construct their own personal religion, one "that is right for me." Both modernists and postmodernists are essentially godless. The Deism of the Enlightenment has morphed into what has been called moralistic therapeutic Deism. God is distant and detached from His creation,

---

18 See Betz, *After Enlightenment*, 255, who quotes and discusses Hamann's explanation of the "mystery of language" in terms of the *communicatio idiomatum*, the doctrine in Lutheran Christology dealing with the communication between the two natures of Christ.

but in today's version, He still cares and offers therapy to help solve your problems. As postmodernists construct their own religions, they might project a more mystical kind of god, but one who is not too demanding and who accords with their desires.

If, as Betz says, Hamann's way is the only alternative to nihilism, and if Hamann's way is ordinary Lutheranism, this would suggest that ordinary Lutheranism can be particularly relevant to ordinary modernists and postmodernists.

THIS BOOK

Modernity drained the outside world of its significance. So post-modernity sent people inward. And yet the outside world keeps impinging itself, even on those who think they construct their own reality. Death, for example, is not a personal or cultural construction. It is a reality outside the self. So are suffering, disease, and failure. These come to us from the outside, apart from our will or our power. Good things come to us from the outside too: love, the birth of a child, the sunset over the mountains. These are all objective, physical realities. However much our philosophy might tell us that these things—love, children, sunsets—are meaningless, we know that they are not. However much our philosophy might tell us that morality is a matter of our choice and that there are no moral absolutes, we do not really believe that. Otherwise, why do we still feel guilt and shame and indignation? Why are we always trying to justify ourselves?

One thing that we need, both to deliver us from the reductionisms of modernity and the alienated subjectivity of postmodernity, is a way to recover the spiritual significance of objective reality. Lutheranism—with its emphasis on creation, incarnation, sacraments, and vocation—can help us do that. Other religions dismiss the world as an illusion, and other theologies promise to help us leave behind the physical world so we can be more spiritual. But Lutheranism shows how the physical realm and the most ordinary corners of our lives—our work, our families, and our society in all of its secularity—are charged with the presence of God. And it shows that our endless attempts at self-justification—proving to others and to ourselves that we are right—are unnecessary. Because we are justified by Christ. Lutheranism can also help people today regain a conception of God, come to terms with suffering, and gain a sense that their lives have meaning.

Lutheranism shows how the physical realm and the most ordinary corners of our lives—our work, our families, and our society in all of its secularity—are charged with the presence of God.

It may be that Lutheranism is an articulation of Christianity that can reach relativists, secularists, the spiritual but not religious, those who cannot so much as conceive of God, those who try to turn themselves into God, and other products and casualties of contemporary culture.

CHAPTER I

INTRODUCTION: MEGA-CHURCH OR METACHURCH?

Five hundred years after the outbreak of the Protestant Reformation, there is the sense that twenty-first century Christianity could use another Reformation. Contemporary churches seem adrift, confused, and dysfunctional, ill-equipped for the challenges of secularism, postmodernism, and cultural change. Many Christians believe that churches need to make changes in order to reach the "unchurched," including the growing number of those who describe themselves as "spiritual but not religious."

But could it be that the same theology that ignited the Reformation five hundred years ago could bring reformation to the church of the twenty-first century? Or, even more difficult, offer an articulation of Christianity that would resonate with postmodernists, secularists, and those who are "spiritual but not religious"?

> *Could it be that the same theology that ignited the Reformation five hundred years ago could bring reformation to the church of the twenty-first century?*

BURNED-OUT BELIEVERS AND SPIRITUAL SECULARISTS

There is a growing need to recover authentic Christian spirituality that can engage both nonbelievers and burned-out believers. Countless people have given up on the church; they know enough to know they do not want to know any more. Some perceive churches to be groups of narrow-minded, inauthentic people who gather together weekly to cast judgment on their neighbors. Some liken churches to timeshare presentations in which unsuspecting people are lured in by free doughnuts and entertainment only to be hit up with a request for money. Others consider churches to be dusty social clubs where grandma goes to play pinochle. Some are veterans of megachurches but come to the point of thinking, "Is that all there is"? Others have invested themselves wholeheartedly into a particular church or a series of churches, only to become exhausted, spiritually drained, and disillusioned.

These burned-out and disaffected believers are often still on church rolls, but many have joined the rising number of people who do not identify with any religious affiliation. Known as the "nones," this group constitutes one-fifth of the American public.[1] There is an even greater concentration of these disaffected believers among millennials (young adults who grew up in the period of transition between the twentieth and twenty-first centuries). One-third of adults under thirty do not identify with any religious affiliation.[2] This phenomenon is certainly not limited to North America; many parts of Europe outpace the rest of the world. Regardless, the reality is this: more and more people are attending church less and less.

---

1   Pew Research Center, "'Nones' on the Rise," October 9, 2012, www.pewforum.org/2012/10/09/nones-on-the-rise.

2   Pew Research Center, "'Nones' on the Rise."

Most of these individuals, however, are not strictly atheist or agnostic. While thirteen million people in the United States describe themselves as atheist or agnostic, a staggering thirty-three million simply have no religious affiliation.[3] While not identifying with a particular religious community, these people believe in God, pray often, and deeply desire a life that is rich in spirituality. This group often describes itself as being "spiritual but not religious." They are often concerned with spiritual issues and open to the possibility of the supernatural, but they resist organized religion and often refuse to classify themselves as being members of any particular faith.

The reality is this: more and more people are attending church less and less.

These burned-out believers and spiritual secularists have given up any hope that an engaging and meaningful spirituality can be found in a single Christian denomination. Rather than attending worship at a local church, they prefer attending to their spiritual needs elsewhere. Rather than searching the Scriptures, they prefer to search the metaphysics aisle at their local bookstore. Instead of being fed by a single denomination, they prefer to feast on a smorgasbord of spiritual beliefs. These disaffected believers have not rejected the existence of God or the need for meaningful spirituality; however, they have strongly rejected whatever it is they think churches today have to offer.

To be certain, churches have sought to engage the "unchurched." The Church Growth Movement advocates being "seeker-sensitive," which often means it relies heavily on gimmicks and glitz. The goal is to eliminate church traditions that might be obstacles and unfamiliar to outsiders, thus making the church more attractive to secularists. But this also makes the church more secular. Weak theology

---

3   Pew Research Center, " 'Nones' on the Rise."

is accompanied by strong coffee served up in an ultramodern build-ing. Worship consists of five praise songs, the sermon resembles a TED Talk, and the prayers all have background music. The emerging church, on the other hand, has sought to engage the same people in a very different way. This movement has attempted to deconstruct the institutional church and free it from outmoded practices, such as worshiping in a traditional church sanctuary, Law and Gospel sermons, and closed Communion—even denominations might seem outdated. Pubs and living rooms are the new sanctuaries. Sermons are light on universal truth claims and heavy on open dia-logue. "Generous orthodoxy," a radical openness and acceptance of widely different teachings, is considered the most effective way to engage disaffected believers. Potlucks are rebranded as "communal eating."

These efforts have worked to an extent. The Church Growth and the Emerging Church Movements have engaged a number of people with the Gospel of Jesus Christ. However, there is serious doubt about exactly how effective they have been and will continue to be in the future when it comes to transmitting Christianity in its richness and depth.[4]

And there is considerable doubt about how effective these efforts are at engaging burned-out and disaffected believers thirty years old and younger, many of whom are casualties of trendy youth groups and accommodating megachurches. The millennial generation is quite adept at sniffing out anything that is inauthentic or phony. They can hear laugh tracks from a mile away. They can sense when someone is too old for skinny jeans. And they know when a church

---

4   See, for example, Gary L. Macintosh, ed., *Evaluating the Church Growth Movement: Five Views* (Grand Rapids, MI: Zondervan, 2010); Gregory A. Pritchard, *Willow Creek Seeker Services: Evaluating a New Way of Doing Church* (Grand Rapids, MI: Baker, 1996); Lucas V. Woodford, *Great Commission, Great Confusion, or Great Confession? The Mission of the Holy Christian Church* (Eugene, OR: Wipf & Stock, 2012).

is putting on an act. Is continually updating the church culture so that it accords with the nonchurch culture the best framework for recovering authentic Christian spirituality? Our contention is no.

On the most pragmatic level, the strategy of continually making minor stylistic "improvements" as a way to become more effective works only to a point, and then it stops working. This can be seen in computer programming with the problem of the "local maximum."[5]

Although a simple task, sorting numbers is a benchmark test in the field of computer programming. A programming language is judged on the basis of how many steps it takes to organize one hundred numbers. Programmers load a random set of one hundred numbers into a computer and see how efficiently the programming language puts those numbers in order.

Is continually updating the church culture so that it accords with the nonchurch culture the best framework for recovering authentic Christian spirituality?

Computer scientist Danny Hallis devised a unique plan to break the record for this benchmark test. At the time Hallis began his work, the world record was set at sixty-six steps. He developed a software program that created thousands of algorithmic miniprograms. These miniprograms were then tested to see if they showed any capacity for sorting numbers. If they were able to sort numbers, then they survived into the next generation and were bred with another one of the miniprograms. This process was repeated a few thousand times until it had made a program that could sort the numbers in seventy-five steps. This was pretty impressive for a first attempt. However, no matter how many times Hallis ran the experiment, it continually stalled out in the range of seventy-five steps.

---

5   For another explanation and application of the principle, see Seth Godin's blogpost, "Understanding Local Max," *Seth's Blog*, November 9, 2005, http://sethgodin.typepad.com/seths_blog/2005/11/understanding_l.html.

There was a problem: The system had reached a local maximum.

Imagine placing all these programs on a landscape. The least efficient programs (99–80 steps) would be in the low valleys, and the most efficient programs (79–75 steps) would be on the high ridges. Since the system only rewarded programs that improved on the prior generation, there was no incentive for a program to step backward and run the risk of death. A program would simply continue in a similar arrangement in order to remain on top of a high ridge. This meant that they seldom made further improvements once they had reached the top of a ridge. Since it had created a program more effective than all the others, it stalled out as if it had made the most effective program possible. In other words, the system treated a high ridge as if it were Mount Everest.

Hallis devised a solution to overcome these local maximums. He introduced "predators" into the system. A miniprogram could not remain at a high ridge without the threat of being destroyed by one of these predators. Thus, the miniprograms had to constantly seek improvements in order to stay alive. After resolving the issue of local maximums, Hallis ran the experiment again. This time the result was stunning: sixty-two steps.

What does this example have to do with churches today? Churches today have hit a local maximum in their efforts to engage the nonchurched.

Let's unpack this a little bit.

Suppose a church began swapping out their printed hymnals for digital screens. They found that this change was effective for engaging unchurched people in the community. In fact, even some young people began showing up on Sunday. The church then decided to construct a coffee shop in the narthex. This addition was also effective for engaging a

Churches today have hit a local maximum in their efforts to engage the nonchurched.

number of disaffected individuals. Seeing how both of these efforts were effective, they merged them together by bringing the coffee shop into the worship space and utilizing the screens more often. They improved on this program little by little: more coffee machines, more froth and foam, a wider selection of praise music, and bigger screens with more pixels. Bit by bit, they built on this paradigm until the screens were as big as possible and their coffee shop rivaled any business in town. They had hit a local maximum: they were the church with the best coffee and the biggest screens.

Does this mean that they had discovered the most effective means of reaching the unchurched? Hardly. People could easily go to another coffee shop in town and get a cup of fair-trade, pour-over coffee without all the ruckus of a praise band. People could go to the movie theater and see a screen with higher resolution and comfier chairs. The program that this church was running could only take them so far. It was certainly effective in its own terms. Nevertheless, they had only ascended to the top of a ridge, bringing in a certain number of new people, but doing little to spread Christianity through the culture as a whole.

The same thing goes for the Emerging Church Movement. Creating a worshiping community that is free from the authoritarian dogma of the past can be effective for engaging postmodern generations. Open dialogue and generous hospitality are enticing for disaffected believers. Fully inked pub churches will certainly provide a safe space for spiritual conversation.

Still, this program will inevitably reach a local maximum. Third spaces are present everywhere, and people can find authentic community just as easily at the barbershop. Public universities are hard to compete with when it comes to rejecting the authoritarian dogmas of the past. Someone looking for tattooed biceps and gnarly beards can find more than enough at the local dive bar. The emerging church has found something that is effective in attracting the attention of some people who are unchurched or alienated believers. Yet, it has only worked its way to the top of a ridge.

The various techniques proposed for "growing the church" gained recognition because they seemed more effective than previous efforts. They "improved" on previous practices and found ways to bring more people into church. Yet, like the computer programs, they can only go so far. In order to achieve their mission, both computer programs and churches need to confront the "predators." For Christianity, those would be sin and death, or, put another way, the world, the flesh, and the devil. Instead of tinkering with style, for better or worse, churches need to deal, in a serious way, with the content of their teaching. Specifically, they need to find effective ways to rescue people from their life-and-death spiritual problems, particularly those that are characteristic of our age.

We need a different framework. We need a better framework. We need to recognize that these past movements have maximized their effectiveness. We need a framework that can move beyond these local maximums and engage the thirty-three million people who are spiritual but not religious. Rather than pushing for bigger screens and skinnier jeans, we believe churches today need a framework that will allow us to recover authentic Christian spirituality. No sociological studies for being "seeker sensitive." No wishy-washy dialogue that refuses to assert anything of substance. No new blends of coffee or complimentary tablets behind every pew. We simply need a way to recover authentic Christian spirituality.

Imagine if it were possible for churches today to engage people with a real and powerful Christianity that is not predicated on new gimmicks, cultural conformity, or downplaying doctrine. What if churches could offer a robust spirituality that is not a mile wide and an inch deep? What would it look like if churches had a framework for engaging burned-out and disaffected believers while still remaining faithful?

This framework would have to be authentically Christian. The nearness of God through the incarnation of Jesus Christ is authentically Christian. Divine justification leading to an existence that is affirmed by God is authentically Christian. Vocation bringing together the secular and spiritual realms is authentically Christian. These notions were not concocted by sociologists or some Seattle-based baristas; they are historically rooted truths of the Christian faith. They are based in and flow out of the Gospel of Jesus Christ. Rather than being a protean blob that morphs with the culture, this framework would be a uniquely Christian expression. Instead of being a product of the ever-changing zeitgeist, this framework would be authentically Christian at its core.

Imagine a Christianity of Christianities. Not just Baptist spirituality, Roman Catholic spirituality, but one that draws on the genius of all Christian traditions. The strongest elements from every different Christian heritage could be emphasized, while avoiding their weaknesses. Rather than diluting the diversity of Christianity into a vague, indistinct mess (as in last century's Ecumenical Movement), this approach would hold the tensions together and maintain their integrity. Along the lines of what G. K. Chesterton describes in *Orthodoxy*, this framework would be adept at "combining furious opposites, by keeping them both, and keeping them both furious."[6] It would draw together many different paradoxes from across the panoply of Christian traditions and "give room for good things to run wild."[7] And yet, rather than being an ecumenical lowest common denominator, it would have its own distinctives that directly address the needs and issues of our day.

---

6   G.K. Chesterton, *Orthodoxy* (New York: SnowBall Classics Publishing, 2015), 60.

7   Chesterton, *Orthodoxy*, 61.

This framework would be markedly better than the Church Growth or Emerging Church Movements. Stronger than a double shot of espresso, this framework would hold together the strengths of many different Christian traditions. Clearer than any high-resolution screen, this framework would convey the eternal truth of the Christian faith. Louder than any praise band, this different approach would speak to burned-out and disaffected believers trying to make sense of a secular, postmodern world.

There is, in fact, a theology at hand that could help us build this framework. It is called Lutheran Christianity.

METACHURCH

Martin Luther's nailing of his Ninety-Five Theses against the sale of indulgences on the church door in Wittenberg on October 31, 1517, was a pivotal moment in history, a transition point between the premodern and the modern eras. But Luther, who has been variously described both as the last medieval man and as the first modern man, bridges the eras.

Luther's project was not to break away from but to reform the one true Church. He thought that the essential message of the Church—that Christ died to save sinners—had become buried under institutional preoccupation with power, moral corruption, and theological additions that had the effect of obscuring the Gospel. His immediate objection in 1517 was to a penitential system that encouraged Christians to pay their way out of purgatory. Essentially, this system said, "You can either spend thousands of years in the fires of purgatory, where you would pay the 'temporal' penalty for your sins, even for sins that were atoned for and forgiven, confessed and absolved. Or, you can pay the church for an indulgence, which applies the merits of the saints (not Christ) to your account." In the consequent debates over the issue, defenders of indulgences asserted the pope's authority to impose such a system. Luther countered by asserting the Bible's greater authority. As the controversy over indulgences continued to build, more and more issues came into play, including those that had long scandalized faithful Christians (such as the pope's claims to secular rule, enforced by the papal army; Rome's moral decadence, with some popes making archbishops out of their illegitimate children; and the bribery required for major church offices; among other issues). But the pope stood his ground, refusing to make even the most obviously justified reforms. He excommunicated Luther and his followers, who nevertheless kept gathering for worship. Christendom had already been split between West and East, and now Western Christianity was divided too.

And yet, Luther was successful, to a certain extent, in reforming the Church of Rome. In an attempt to combat the Protestants, the Council of Trent did address the financial corruption and moral degradation that gave the Protestants so much ammunition. And it did promote measures to increase the personal piety of Catholic Christians. For those reformations, Roman Catholics owe Luther a debt of gratitude. But the Council of Trent doubled down on the theological issues, insisting on the authority of the pope, the role of good works in salvation, and the necessity of the penitential system. The council did stop the *sale* of indulgences, but they still retained indulgences. The church would reduce time in purgatory for acts of piety, such as going on prescribed pilgrimages or performing specified acts of devotion, but not for a commercial transaction.

Meanwhile, charges came against Luther from his own Protestant side of the divide saying that he "didn't go far enough," meaning he didn't remove from the church everything that could be seen as remotely "Catholic." Later Protestants turned the Reformation into a revolution. New Protestants criticizing Luther subsequently minimized the Sacraments, threw out the liturgy, burned the cruci-fixes, and developed their own theologies based on their own inter-pretations of Scripture. New ways of being Christian would prolif-erate, leading to the plethora of denominations that characterizes Protestantism today.

But Luther's Reformation of five hundred years ago was different from those Protestant revolutions that would soon follow. His goal was to reform the Church, not demolish it and build something better on its ruins. He did not want to start a new church, but to reform the only Church that existed. He sought to correct abuses that thought-ful Christians throughout the Middle Ages also criticized. (Notice how Dante and Chaucer also attacked the sale of indulgences.) He sought to recenter the Church on its essential message: namely, that God became flesh in Jesus Christ, who died to take away the sins of the world and who rose again from the dead for our salvation.

Luther interpreted virtually everything in the church in light of this Good News. This is the message of the Word of God, which the Holy Spirit uses to convict us of our sin and to reveal to us our Savior, thus creating faith in our hearts. This is the significance of the Sacra-ments—Holy Communion and Holy Baptism—which are not mer-itorious acts on our part, but means by which Christ connects us to Himself. This Good News, this Gospel, is communicated in the his-toric liturgy and in congregational singing, in the Rite of Confession and Absolution and in the Office of the Holy Ministry. This Gospel creates faith, which bears fruit in love and service to our neighbors in the vocations—in the family, the workplace, and the society—of ordinary life.

Luther was addressing the Church as a whole. He had a *cath-olic* vision, from the Greek words meaning "with respect to the whole." Since Roman Catholics have claimed that term in a way that excludes Protestants and Orthodox, perhaps we can adopt another word: metatheology.

The prefix *meta* has become postmodernist jargon for "self-referential," as in a novel about the author writing the novel, or a movie about the making of the movie. More usefully, *meta* means "about," in the sense of a consideration of the entire category. *Metadata* means data about data (its source, how the data was collected, etc.). *Metahistory* means a history of histories (the unfolding of different theories of history, from chronicles of facts, through stories of "great" human beings, through analysis of impersonal social forces). One of the first to use *meta* in this way appears to have been the hero of our Prologue, J. G. Hamann![8] Responding to Kant's *Critique of Pure Reason*, Hamann wrote *Metacritique of the Purism of Reason*.[9] In this "critique of a critique," Hamann indicted Kant for his "Gnostic hatred for the material," exalting abstract reason cut off from experience, history, language, and revelation.[10] Thus as early as 1784, as embodied in one of its greatest thinkers, the Lutheran tradition was going *meta*.

So Lutheranism entails a "metatheology," a theology of theology. All theology must derive not from the Church's human leadership nor from human reason but from the Word of God. This is the "formal principle," the source and authority for theology. The "material principle" is the central

> *All theology must derive not from the Church's human leadership nor from human reason but from the Word of God.*

---

8   Oxford Dictionaries, https://en.oxforddictionaries.com/definition/metacritique, credits Hamann for the first use of "metacritique." The word's appearance in Hamann's book on Kant would have been in 1784. This date is earlier than any of those cited in the Oxford English Dictionary's entry for the prefix *meta* in this sense.

9   See Hoon Lee, "Metacritique: Hamann on Kant's Three Purisms," *Exploring Church History: Reflections on History and Theology*, December 4, 2014. Accessed February 8, 2017. exploringchurchhistory.com/metacritique-hamann-kants-three-purisms.

10   Quoted in Lee, "Metacritique: Hamann on Kant's Three Purisms."

content of that theology. That would be our justification by God's grace through faith in the work of Jesus Christ. And the Church of Luther's Reformation entails a "metachurch," a church of churches.

Like Roman Catholicism and Eastern Orthodoxy, Lutheranism is *sacramental*. In teaching regeneration in the waters of Baptism and the actual presence of Christ's body and blood in Holy Communion, Lutheranism—like these other major Christian traditions—sees a close connection between the spiritual and the physical. As in Roman Catholicism and Eastern Orthodoxy, Lutheran churches worship *liturgically*, employing historic rites that testify to the objective holiness and grace to be found in the Divine Service.

But like Protestantism, Lutheranism is *biblical* and *evangelical*. As we have seen, the Bible and the Gospel are preeminent in Lutheran theology and practice. But, for the Lutheran metachurch, the sacramental and the liturgical are by no means opposed to the biblical and the evangelical, as is usual in both the Catholic and the Protestant traditions. Lutheran sacramental theology derives from a literal reading of the Bible; the Word of God attached to a visible element is what makes a sacrament; the Bible is itself, in effect, a sacrament, in which the Holy Spirit is truly present to create faith. The liturgy consists largely of reciting, chanting, and hearing the Word of God. And Lutheran worship, though liturgical, makes strong use of the characteristic Protestant elements of worship; namely, preaching and the congregational singing of hymns.

Even with the proliferation of Protestant theologies after Luther's Reformation, the churches that followed and developed his theology continued their *meta* quality, in the sense of giving a bigger perspective that contains the rest. Thus, the first major Protestant alternative to Lutheranism, the so-called Reformed churches, soon split into the two warring and mutually contradictory strains of Calvinism and Arminianism. From a Lutheran point of view, each took passages of Scripture—respectively, those that speak of God's agency in salvation and those that speak of human agency—and constructed a theology around them. This, however, necessitated explaining away the contrary passages. Lutheran theology, in contrast, adheres closely to the text of Scripture even in its paradoxes and even when it confounds human understanding. The Lutheran metachurch can thus keep the polarities of Calvinism and Arminianism, as well as other theologies, in suspension.

Lutheran theology, in contrast, adheres closely to the text of Scripture even in its paradoxes and even when it confounds human understanding.

Like Calvinists, Lutherans emphasize the grace of God, that faith and salvation come sheerly as His gift. Lutheran theology also speaks of election and predestination. And yet Lutheranism avoids the darker implications of Calvinism, such as double predestination (God's election to damnation) and the uncertainty over election (the possibility given by the Calvinist doctrine of the limited atonement that Christ did not die for me). Like Arminianism, Lutherans emphasize that Christ's atonement is universal, that He died for the sins of the world and not just for the elect. Lutherans also agree with Arminians that salvation can be lost, that a perseverance in unrepented sin can make faith die. But instead of focusing on the power of the will, as Arminians do, in "making a decision" for Christ and in the convert's ability to live without sin, Lutherans continue to stress the Christian's continual need for God's grace that is active in the Gospel.

What reconciles these seeming contradictions is Lutheran sacramentalism. Christ died for all, and all have access to His saving work by receiving the Word and the Sacraments. Calvinists, ironically, believe in eternal security, and yet they often feel insecure because they have no way of knowing whether they are of the elect. Lutherans believe salvation can be lost—not all of the baptized or the converted persevere in the faith—and yet they emphasize the assurance of salvation, which comes from receiving the Word and the Sacraments.

This metachurch quality can also be seen in the relationship of Lutheranism to other strains and motifs of Christianity. Lutheranism affirms the Christian intellectual tradition, putting a high value on education and making historical contributions to the arts and culture. And yet, it rejects rationalism and promotes individual piety. Just as today's charismatics stress a personal supernatural experience through various "spiritual gifts," Lutherans stress a personal supernatural experience through partaking of the gifts given in the Sacraments. Lutherans agree with the Anabaptists that the church is to be separate from the world in a way that also agrees with the social activists who say that Christians should make the world a better place. From its inception, Lutheranism has been both revolutionary and conservative, individualistic and collective. The Lutheran spiritual heritage can help to inform and reconcile all of the other traditions that it, in a sense, gave birth to, as well as the early and medieval traditions that gave birth to Lutheranism.

The Lutheran spiritual heritage can help to inform and reconcile all of the other traditions that it, in a sense, gave birth to, as well as the early and medieval traditions that gave birth to Lutheranism.

But such a metachurch is not "ecumenical" in the sense of the modernist Ecumenical Movement of the last century, nor in the postmodern relativism that embraces diversity for its own sake. Instead of trying to achieve Christian unity by minimizing the distinctives of the various Christian traditions, downplaying doctrine, and minimizing the supernatural, Lutheran Christianity emphasizes them.

Consider the difference in approach between Lutherans and Anglicans, another major group of sacramental, liturgical Protestants. Anglicans, with whom Lutherans have many historical connections, cultivate a "middle way" between Catholicism and

Protestantism. They do so by accommodating a wide range of beliefs, phrasing their doctrinal statements on the Sacraments, for example, so that members with a Catholic, a Calvinist, or an Evangelical background could find agreement and commune in good conscience. Lutherans, though, define their teachings with great precision. They look for unity not so much in common worship as the Anglicans do—indeed, Lutherans, while liturgical, allow for a range of practices—but in doctrinal agreement.[11]

Instead of trying to achieve Christian unity by minimizing the distinctives of the various Christian traditions, downplaying doctrine, and minimizing the supernatural, Lutheran Christianity emphasizes them.

As a metachurch, Lutheran Christianity has its own distinctives, which grow out of its comprehensive nature.

From a Lutheran perspective, Catholics are not nearly catholic *enough*. Ever since the Council of Trent, they have excluded all Protestants from their catholicity. Modern Catholicism has begun to recognize that Protestants can be Christians, but they are still outside the church unless they come back under the authority of the pope.

Similarly, charismatics are not nearly charismatic *enough*. The word *charisma* is Greek for "gift." Christianity is indeed about the gifts of the gracious God. But charismatics look inside themselves, to the Holy Spirit within, to give them ecstatic tongues, revelations, and miraculous powers. But for Lutherans, God's supernatural gifts of faith, salvation, and the Holy Spirit come from the outside, through the objective gifts of God's Word and Christ's Sacraments.

---

11 "For the true unity of the Church it is enough to agree about the doctrine of the Gospel and the administration of the Sacraments. It is not necessary that human traditions, that is, rites or ceremonies instituted by men, should be the same everywhere. As Paul says, 'One Lord, one faith, one baptism, one God and Father of all' (Ephesians 4:5–6)" (Augsburg Confession, Article VII, paragraphs 2–4).

Similarly, Evangelicals are not nearly evangelical *enough*. The word *evangelical* derives from the Latin word for "gospel." Just as Calvinists go by the name *Reformed*, Lutherans in Europe would go by the name *Evangelical*. That is a much better name for this metachurch, since the Gospel—rather than the thought of a particular man—is at the center of all of its teachings. But now, especially in the English-speaking world, evangelicals are all Christians who believe in personal conversion and the Bible. But they often reserve the Gospel for that moment of conversion. After that, they tend to put themselves back under the Law. For Lutheran evangelicals, on the other hand, the Gospel of Christ's forgiveness is something Christians must keep returning to.

Lutherans, therefore, are the metacatholics, the metacharismatics, and the metaevangelicals.

ISSUES FOR THE NEW REFORMATION

So how might this metachurch spark a Reformation for the twenty-first century as it did five hundred years ago? What are the issues in the church and in society that need reforming? This will be the topic for the rest of this book, but let us mention a few.

First, the fundamental problem of the twenty-first century, as every century, is sin. And the solution is the cross of Christ. But Western society today has worldviews, cultural trends, and blind spots that make it difficult for people to recognize their sinfulness. And churches themselves have worldviews, cultural trends, and blind spots of their own that hinder them from effectively proclaiming the cross of Christ.

The Distortion of God. The very idea of God is distorted in the twenty-first century. For various reasons we shall discuss, God has been banished from the realm of objective, ordinary reality. Secularists imagine that they can do without Him completely. But even those who do believe in God often think of Him in one of two ways: as either utterly transcendent, to the point of abstraction and irrelevance—as in the moralistic therapeutic Deism that prevails among teenagers and young adults; or, as with many Christians, as dwelling within, to the point of sometimes confusing Him with themselves.

Largely missing, even in the teachings of many churches, is the distinct Christian insight: God has become incarnate in Jesus Christ. He took on human flesh. He lived a human life in the real, objective, physical world. And the incarnate Son of God is still present with His people. To be sure, all Christians affirm the incarnation and the deity of Christ, and yet this teaching is often pushed to the margins today or buried beneath teachings with a higher priority. But Lutheran Christianity makes this essential teaching of all Christianity absolutely central. And Lutheran sacramentalism, which emphasizes Christ's real presence in the physical elements, is a constant reminder and reinforcement of the truth of God's objective presence.

The Gnostic Heresy. Related to the imagined banishment of God—of course, He has not actually been banished but remains where He has always been—is the overall denigration of the objective, physical realm. This is ironic, since many secularists today believe the physical realm is all that exists. But they deny that it has any meaning, apart from the subjective meanings that we may give it. Postmodernists deny the possibility of objective truth altogether, insisting that what seems true is only a personal or a cultural construction. Furthermore, postmodernists also deny the possibility of objective moral standards. As a social construction, morality is nothing more than an imposition of power. Individuals, however, can "choose" their own moral code, deciding what is right "for them."

All of this amounts to a resurgence of the Gnostic heresy. Teaching that a demon, not God, created the universe and denying that Jesus Christ has come "in the flesh" (1 John 4:1–3), the Gnostics rejected the spiritual significance of the physical world, including the body. Although sometimes this rejection of the physical manifested itself in ascetic denial of God's gifts (1 Timothy 4:1–5), it also manifested itself in complete moral license, since, according to Gnosticism, what we do in the body has nothing to do with our spiritual state (in contrast, see 1 Corinthians 6:12–20). In its hyperspirituality, Gnosticism taught that salvation had to do with acquiring an elite hidden knowledge (*gnosis*), with Jesus being one of many spirit guides.

Scholars have studied the implicit Gnostic elements in American religion, but many liberal theologians are explicitly embracing Gnosticism as a "suppressed" alternative to orthodox Christianity. This is especially true of feminist theologians.[12] They feel that by denying the spiritual significance of the body, Gnosticism gives support for women's ordination, women's full equality with men, and the overall irrelevance of sex and gender. Today's popular Gnosticism is evident in transgenderism—the view that a person's gender identity is separate from the body—as well as sexual immorality, the rejection of procreation, the "transhumanist" project of replacing the body with technology, and indifference to nature and natural law.

In his book *The American Religion*, Harold Bloom maintains that all religions that originated in America—Mormonism, Christian Science, new age spirituality—and also American-made versions of Christianity—Seventh Day Adventism, Jehovah's Witnesses, Pentecostalism, Southern Baptists, and Fundamentalism—are essentially Gnostic.[13] Bloom, who considers himself a Gnostic, identifies three

---

12 See the work of Elaine Pagels, especially *The Gnostic Gospels* (New York: Vintage Books, 1979).

13 Harold Bloom, *The American Religion*, (New York: Chu Hartley Publishers, 2006). He shows that each of these American religions in some way downplays the physical realm in favor of a higher "spiritual" state. They also claim to disclose some knowledge that has previously been hidden. And, in some cases, such as Mormonism and the New Age Movement, they even employ narratives that are similar to the ancient Gnostic myths.

groups that opposed this Gnosticism: Jews, Catholics, and Lutherans.

And so it can be today: Lutherans—with their understanding of creation, incarnation, God's presence in the Sacraments, His governance of the world, and His involvement in human vocations—can bring back not only belief in God but also belief in reality.

Confusion and Repudiation of Law and Gospel. The Gnostic assumptions of postmodernism undermine any kind of objective moral order, so that it has become difficult for many people today even to conceive of moral absolutes. They really believe that they create their own morality. They are "pro-choice" when it comes to abortion, so whether a woman keeps the baby or kills it, it is right "for her," as long as she freely choses the outcome. That ethic of choice is also evident in other moral issues today, from euthanasia to human relationships. People still have a moral sensibility—God's Law is written on their hearts, after all (Romans 2:15)—but they displace it away from God's commands toward their own causes. Above all, they formulate a personal morality that is easier for them to keep. It might be based on attitudes, political beliefs, and benevolent feelings. Its good works may consist of recycling, voting correctly, and acts of tolerance. Ironically, although people today may be sexually promiscuous and violate other tenets of "traditional morality," they still insist that "I am a good person." They are self-righteous without being righteous. Thus, they manage to be religious legalists. If they think in these terms, they are likely to believe they deserve to go to heaven because of their goodness.

It is difficult for churches today to deal with these immoral moralists because the churches, too, are often confused about the Law and the Gospel. Many churches today only preach the Law, making Christianity a matter of personal behavior. But they do so by turning the Gospel into Law, turning faith in Christ into something a person has to *do*, or, in accord with postmodernism, something one has to *choose*. Other churches do preach the Gospel, but only for conversion, then encouraging Christians to put their trust in the Law after all. Still others preach the Gospel in such a way that the Law has *no* bearing on the Christian life at all, excusing the whole range of immorality in those who profess faith in Christ. Still others are preaching neither the Law nor the Gospel, substituting "life coach" inspiration, politics, or the prosperity gospel.

Postmodern secularists with not the slightest comprehension of "traditional morality" have no interest in churches when moralism is all they teach. And they do not need the Gospel as a cover for what they feel free to do anyway. Meanwhile, churches confused about the Law and Gospel can neither move secularists to repentance nor effectively apply the life-changing message of Christ.

Lutherans have always cultivated the art of applying God's Law so that it brings conviction of sin. Destroying every shred of self-righteousness, this "theological use" of the Law provokes repentance, awakening sinners to their need for the Gospel, whereupon Lutherans proclaim the Christ who bore their sins and the penalty they deserve. Christ justifies sinners, creating a faith that is active in love and good works. But Christians continue to need both the Law and the Gospel, as they struggle against sin and grow in holiness.

CONFUSIONS ABOUT THE SECULAR WORLD

As H. Richard Niebuhr has shown, Christians have long struggled with the proper relationship between Christianity and culture.[14] Shall we separate from it, conform to it, rule it, or transform it? Today, those options continue according to various theological traditions, but in a curiously confused way. Some Christians separate from the

14   H. Richard Niebuhr, *Christ and Culture* (New York: Harper & Row, 1951).

culture, only to set up Christian sub-cultures that are little different from the culture they are opposing. Liberals conform to the secularist culture to the point of eliminating any distinctively Christian beliefs, while conservatives also conform to the secularist culture in an attempt to get secularists to attend their churches. Both liberals and conservatives dream of ruling or transforming the culture, so that now there is both a social gospel of the left and a social gospel of the right. Thus churches have become highly politicized, identified more by their quest for power than by their proclamation of eternal life through the cross of Christ.

> *Churches have become highly politicized, identified more by their quest for power than by their proclamation of eternal life through the cross of Christ.*

Lutheranism has solved the cultural problem. Its doctrine of the two kingdoms is this: the kingdom of heaven and the kingdom of the world are two distinct spheres that must not be confused with each other. But Christians are citizens of both realms, and God is king of them both, though ruling each in different ways. The secular realm, in all of its secularity, belongs to God, who rules it with His providential care, His created order, and His Law. The spiritual realm is also God's, and He governs it with His Word, His redemption, and His Gospel. Christians are to live out their faith in the world, applying God's moral law by improving the lives of their neighbors and faithfully carrying out their vocations. Meanwhile, they grow in their faith by Word and Sacrament and are prepared for a life that never ends in the kingdom of heaven. The Lutheran doctrine of culture thus shows how a Christian can be "in the world," without being "of the world" (John 17:14–18).

The related doctrine of vocation shows how the ordinary relationships and tasks of life are charged with meaning, as God works in and through our multiple callings in the family, the workplace, the church, and the culture. Instead of our being bored with our mundane lives, the doctrine of vocation can teach us how to appreciate our lives, as God transfigures them with meaning, value, and His presence.

The first Reformation had to do with knowing God rightly, correcting confusions over a spirituality that devalued the world, the confusion of Law and Gospel, the political focus of the church, the relationship of Christianity to culture, and the vocation of Christians in ordinary life. However, these issues may be more heightened today than they were five hundred years ago.

This book will explore these major issues faced by the contemporary church. We will also be addressing them in more personal terms, as they affect individual human beings—both Christians and non-Christians—in their spiritual struggles. Consider the following catalog of religious difficulties today and how Lutheran Christianity addresses them.

❖ To those who cannot conceive of religious abstractions, Lutheran Christianity focuses on God incarnate in human flesh, who makes Himself known through tangible means and is truly present in words, water, bread, and wine.

❖ To those who believe all religions, institutions, and values are nothing more than the assertion of power, Lutheran Christianity stresses a God who lays aside His almighty power, to be born in a manger and to die on a cross, making Himself known in weakness by human beings in their weakness.

❖ To those who believe their lives are meaningless, Lutheran Christianity offers the doctrine of vocation, teaching that God is present, though hidden, in the work and relationships of ordinary life.

❖ To those put off by a Christianity they associate with legalistic demands and moral requirements, which they have neither the ability nor the desire to fulfill, Lutheran Christianity offers a nonmoralistic religion, one in which God accomplishes everything necessary for salvation. Whereupon, the moral life is recast, going from external compliance to rules to loving and serving your neighbor in vocation (in the family, the workplace, the church, and the society).

❖ To those put off by a church preoccupied with politics, Lutheran Christianity distinguishes between the spiritual kingdom (the main business of the church) and the earthly kingdom (in which we have a vocation as citizens), thus affirming our civic responsibilities without making them our ultimate concerns.

❖ To those who feel religion to be a burden, Lutheran Christianity proclaims the freedom of the Christian.

❖ To those who yearn for spirituality but do not find it in rationalistic dogmas and bureaucratic institutions, Lutheran Christianity offers mystery, paradox, worship centered in the real presence of Christ in the Sacraments, and the spiritual heritage of the historic Church.

❖ To those who are confused and scandalized by the divisions in the Church and do not know which tradition is the correct one, Lutheran Christianity is uniquely comprehensive, being both evangelical and catholic, holding to both the Word and the Sacraments, resolving, too, such Protestant divisions as Calvinist and Arminian, Baptist and Pentecostal.

❖ To those struggling with family problems and a church that has lost its credibility to speak on such issues due to the plague of divorce and unfaithfulness, Lutheran Christians have a track record of revitalizing the institution of marriage through the doctrine of vocation.

❖ To those who are suffering, Lutheran Christianity repudiates both the prosperity gospel and the Deistic god who looks down from a distance on his tormented creation and does nothing about it. Instead, in its theology of the cross, Lutheran Christianity proclaims a God who takes the griefs of the entire world onto Himself, and who draws near to those who suffer in His own suffering.

❖ To those who are relativists, Lutheran Christianity breaks the pattern of ideological constructions and self-justification, pointing to the One who creates and the One who justifies.

DISCUSSION QUESTIONS

1. Can you relate to being either a burned-out believer or a spiritual secularist? Do changes of worship style reach you? Why or why not?

2. What will a church that encompasses the whole range of Christianity—from Catholic through Protestant—look like? How will it be criticized from the various partial perspectives?

3. What are some parallels between the time of the Reformation five hundred years ago and today?

CHAPTER 2

RECONSIDERING GOD

Today's secular world is "Godless." As such, it either does without God, leaves God out of consideration, or has nothing to do with God. This is simply what "secular" means. But although the world may be Godless, the human beings who inhabit it are not necessarily. A recent Gallup poll found that 89 percent of Americans believe in God.[1] Europeans are much more irreligious, but 51 percent say they believe in God, with an additional 26 percent saying they believe in some kind of spirit or life force.[2] The problem is that people today, both believers and nonbelievers, have difficulty imagining God. Their conception of God tends to be confused, simplistic, and quite different from what is disclosed in the Bible. They have difficulty conceiving of a God who is connected with the world.

---

1 Frank Newport, "Most Americans Still Believe in God," *Gallup Polls*, June 29, 2016, www.gallup.com/poll/193271/americans-believe-god.aspx.

2 TNS Opinion & Social, *Special Eurobarometer 73.1: Biotechnology* (Brussells, Belgium: European Commision, 2010), 203. Accessed June 16, 2017, web.archive.org/web/20101215001129/http://ec.europa.eu/public_opinion/archives/ebs/ebs_341_en.pdf.

Today, both those who believe in God and those who do not believe in God tend to imagine Him as a being who is either utterly transcendent, far above the universe, *or* as a spiritual presence within themselves. Either way, the world and the mundane realities of everyday life are largely bereft of God's presence.

The biblical revelation of God is more complex than the partial truths human beings are able to grasp by themselves. God *is* utterly transcendent, more so than the Deists and abstract philosophers realize. At the same time, He also *does* dwell within the hearts of His children. But there is another truth that is often forgotten today, one that Lutherans especially emphasize: God became a human being, in the flesh. And He continues to manifest Himself through physical means—the water of Holy Baptism and the bread and wine of Holy Communion—and by filling the world and the most mundane spheres of ordinary life.

Not only that, but He also *acts*. God is not a mere philosophical abstraction we must figure out, or a detached deity whom we must placate by our efforts, or a mysterious spiritual entity to whom we must ascend. Lutheran Christianity emphasizes that God descends to us; He saves us; He makes Himself known.

GOD IN THE CLOUD

We used to think of a cloud as nothing more than a billowy mass of condensed water vapor in the sky. Not anymore. Cloud computing has added an entirely new meaning to this word. Today, the cloud refers to a place where you can store and access data and programs over the internet. Rather than saving a file to your computer, you save it to the cloud. Rather than storing your photos on a physical disc, they are stored in the cloud.

Where is the cloud? It's hard to say. It is somewhere out there.

Maybe it is somewhere up there. Maybe it is with Bigfoot and the Loch Ness Monster. All we really know is that it is not located near us in any real way. That is exactly why it is called the cloud. Just as the clouds in the sky are distant and beyond our grasp, cloud computing stores everything at a distance.

Where do files go when they are saved to the cloud? It's hard to say. They are not located on your computer's hard drive. They are not located on a flash drive or removable disk. They are not physically present. They go somewhere out in the distant reaches of the internet. The files seemingly float around in the cloud until you need them.

To be certain, there are some people who actually understand where files go when they are saved to the cloud. Computer scientists, IT technicians, and other digital diviners know where the files are actually located. They know files are stored on remote servers often thousands of miles away from their computers. These remote servers send and receive data by way of the internet. For instance, Facebook relies on a massive group of servers (known as a server farm) that is located on the edge of the Arctic Circle in Northern Sweden. Although there is a physical location where the files reside, the average user has no idea where it is. For the majority of us, it is all just somewhere out there in the cloud.

DEISM

Modern spirituality imagines God as being somewhere not necessarily in *the cloud* but in the clouds. Just as we do not really know where our files are located when they are stored in the cloud, we do not really know where God is located. He is somewhere out there. He is located somewhere just beyond our grasp. He is distant and far away. He dwells in abstraction and enigma. Perhaps God is located just beyond the clouds in the sky. Perhaps God is just beyond the

Arctic Circle. Wherever God is located, it is certainly not here.

This notion of a distant God is a central tenet of Deism. Although its origins reach back into antiquity, Deism gained prominence throughout Europe during the Age of Enlightenment in the seventeenth and eighteenth centuries. Many influential thinkers during this time—John Locke, Matthew Tindal, Voltaire, Ben Franklin, Thomas Jefferson, and several others—espoused some form of Deism. While maintaining a vague belief in God, Deistic theology parted ways with many core teachings of Christianity: the doctrine of the Trinity, the divinity and miracles of Jesus, and the inerrancy of Scripture. Such teachings derived from divine revelation, but Deism, following the tenets of the Enlightenment, sought to be a religion based on reason alone. Deism held to the belief that God exists without intervening in the world; God made the world and ensured its rationality, but then left it alone.

Voltaire, a French writer known for his sharp wit and even sharper satire, summarized the Deistic belief in God when he wrote, "When His Highness sends a ship to Egypt does he trouble his head whether the rats in the vessel are at their ease or not?"[3] Just as a king is not worried about the varmints in the belly of a ship, God is not concerned with the well-being of individual humans. The great architect of the universe has better things to do than trifle about in human suffering and pain, hopes and fears. Deism depicts God as far away and unfeeling, distant and detached from creation.

OUR MODERN FORM OF DEISM

Building on many core Deistic beliefs, modern spirituality is often described as moralistic therapeutic Deism.[4] There is a

---

3   *Candide*, chapter 30.

4   Christian Smith and Melinda Lundquist Denton, *Soul Searching: The Religious and Spiritual Lives of American Teenagers* (New York: Oxford University Press, 2005), 118–70.

widespread belief among people today that God exists in some form and maintains the hidden workings of the universe. But in a kinder, gentler version of Voltaire's theology, this deity wants people to be good to one another, try their hardest, and enjoy a generally happy life. But He is not "judgmental." His adherents are moralistic, not in the Ten Commandments sense but in the moralism of tolerance and niceness. Nevertheless, there is no need for God to be particularly involved in human life on a daily basis. God is aloof and distant from the world, dwelling somewhere out there and not interfering much with human existence.

According to this modern spirituality, there is one exception to God's otherwise distant demeanor—and that's when a problem arises. When a problem cannot easily be resolved, God is called on to roll up His holy sleeves and get to work. These are the rare occasions when God is needed. And these are the rare and fleeting occasions when God is actually near and present within the world. Finally, after the issue has been resolved, God retreats back into the cloud and waits for the next time He is needed. An example of this was seen in the brief spike in American worship attendance following the terrorist attacks on 9/11. Although there was a substantial increase in church attendance after the attacks, this increase was short-lived and did little to change the religious practices in America.[5] More often, God's help is conceived of in terms of therapy—if we can learn to follow His principles or learn how to be tolerant and good like Him, we will be able to better overcome our mistakes, solve our personal problems, and attain happiness.

There are some serious problems with this modern form of Deism. It is spiritually anemic and leaves people perpetually

---

5   Jeremy E. Uecker, "Religious and Spiritual Responses to 9/11: Evidence from the Add Health Study," *Sociological Spectrum: The Official Journal of the Mid-South Sociological Association* 28, no. 5 (2008): 477–509, www.ncbi.nlm.nih.gov/pmc/articles/PMC3118577.

searching for more. At its very best, this modern form of Deism is like a cup of weak decaf coffee that only arouses the desire for something stronger, bolder, and fully caffeinated. At its very worst, this modern form of Deism leaves people in utter despair as they look out into a vacuous universe wondering where God might possibly be found.

A modern spirituality that relies on a distant and aloof deity will never be satisfying. If God is somewhere in the cloud, then He knows nothing of your life. If God dwells in a distant place, then He knows nothing of human hurt and suffering. He is like a doctor who leaves you in the waiting room for hours only to walk in, prescribe some painkillers to numb the hurt, and then promptly leave. This therapeutic deity is like a psychiatrist you keep going back to, even though you are doing all the talking.

And if God is somewhere in the clouds, then He knows nothing of the depth and breadth of human life. If God only shows up when there is a problem, then He does not know the full richness of humanity. The intricacies of human joy cannot be seen from a million miles away. The colorful beauty of this life is lost when viewed from afar. Dwelling in a distant place, God does not know what it is like to savor the taste of food, smell the earthy aroma of black soil, or gaze at the twinkling beauty of the nighttime sky. The spirituality of modern Deism depicts God as being rather ignorant when it comes to the human experience; He is so far away that He cannot possibly know what it is like to be human.

The image of God dwelling somewhere in the cloud means that He is always distant and just beyond our grasp. And, conversely, this means that humanity is somewhat distant and beyond God's grasp. We cannot comprehend Him nor can He fully comprehend us. *In order for a truly meaningful relationship with God to exist, He must be present and near to humanity.* He must fully and completely know what it means to be human. The chasm separating us from God would have to be bridged. Modern spirituality needs to relocate and re-image God. We must recapture what it means to have a God who is near and present, fully engaged in this world, and completely aware of what it means to be human. This is the God that Lutheranism helps us to know.

THE GOD WITHIN

The Enlightenment needed a god—one knowable only through reason rather than revelation—in order to account for the universe and its orderliness that those early scientists were discovering, from the laws of physics to the design of organisms. Then Darwin offered an account of the origin of species that did without God altogether. Therefore, many assumed that the origin of the universe could also be accounted for without God. The laws of nature ground on without a lawgiver. The evident design in the universe that made it intelligible was excluded in favor of impersonal, random, physical processes. Thus, in the nineteenth century, the Age of Reason mutated into an Age of Materialism. According to this worldview, the material realm is all that exists. Furthermore, the only kind of truth is that which is disclosed by scientific empiricism. Thus, for many thoughtful people, Deism gave way to atheism.

But if there is no God behind the physical universe, even at a distance, and if the universe has no design, then it has no meaning. Yes, nature seems to operate in accord with the laws of physics and mathematics. But this apparent order has no purpose, no intrinsic value, and no significance. The laws of nature are nothing more than meaningless repetitions, like an infinite programming loop.

According to this worldview, meaning can only be found in the realm of human subjectivity—human beings find meaning only within themselves. Such thinking has given us the philosophy of existentialism, which teaches that individuals must create their own meaning. The notion that meaning is a subjective construction is a key assumption of postmodernism, with its skepticism and relativism. It has also contributed to a different conception of God.

Instead of conceptualizing God as filling all things, as the Bible describes (see Ephesians 1:15–23), or as a transcendent being beyond the world, as in Deism, the focus shifted to the God within as the rise of Pietism accompanied the Enlightenment. Thus Christianity began to be seen in terms of experiences, inner feelings, and interior spiritual states.

As the Industrial Revolution spread throughout England, John Wesley's Methodism stressed the importance of a personal conversion initiated by the human will, whereupon Christ would dwell within. With the modernism of the twentieth century in the United States came the Pentecostal Movement, which emphasizes the indwelling Holy Spirit. Such theologies hearken back to the "enthusiasts" of Luther's day, that term meaning literally "a god inside." It is ironic that this purposefully nonrational approach to Christianity rose to prominence during the "Age of Reason." While it is true that God dwells within the human heart, just as He transcends His creation, and while many in these movements exhibited genuine faith in Christ, parts of Christianity were minimized—the Sacraments, the Church, the objectivity of salvation.

Today the notion that God is to be found within the self also has non-Christian versions. Hinduism teaches atman, the deity within. Through meditation and disciplines such as yoga, Hindus learn to detach themselves from this world of illusion, going deeper and deeper into themselves until they achieve a very different kind of enlightenment, in which they become one with atman. In the West, Hinduism has influenced the New Age Movement, which also talks about discovering the god within and affirms the deity of the self.

And half-secularized modes of Hinduism are evident in the vogue of yoga and meditation. Those who are "spiritual but not religious" often reject the trappings of formal religions, whether Christianity or Hindusm, but seek to cultivate spirituality by going inward, assuming that this is where the spiritual realm is to be found.

Pop psychology and the clichés of pop culture continually talk about how we create our own reality and must choose the moral beliefs that are right for us. This accords with the more sophisticated constructivism of the postmodernists. But such notions put the self squarely in the position of God as both creator and lawgiver.

When Christianity is seen as an internal state and as a function of the self, the Christian is thrown on his or her own resources. The relationship with God is often seen as originating in the individual's will. This is in line with the postmodernist emphasis on "choice" in the construction of morality and belief systems, but it also can easily turn into moralism and legalism, in which the believer's status with God is dependent on his or her efforts, good deeds, and religious experience. And because the human will is unstable and the sinful nature keeps manifesting itself, the Christian is often plagued with uncertainty about salvation and God's favor. At the same time, this privatized religion can also be expressed in antinomian license. If the outside world has nothing to do with my faith, then why should my actions or the way I treat others matter? I have a relationship with the God within, and He clearly loves me. So what difference does it make? Certainly, the Christianity of the self has little need for the Church or for other Christians. Since the individual constructs his or her own theology, the creeds and doctrines of historic Christianity have no authority. Individual Christians are essentially on their own. This can create a sense of complacency, but times of trial and suffering can raise recurring questions of "Am I really saved?" or even "Is God real after all, or does He only exist in my head?"

THE NEARNESS OF GOD: INCARNATION

God is neither in the cloud nor in the clouds. He does not dwell in abstraction. He is not in some remote realm, recluse reality, or utterly incomprehensible place beyond our grasp. Nor is He located primarily within the self. Rather, God has drawn near to us in the most intimate way imaginable by taking on human flesh in Christ Jesus: "And the Word became flesh and dwelt among us, and we have seen His glory, glory as of the only Son from the Father, full of grace and truth" (John 1:14).

God has drawn near to us through Jesus Christ. Therefore, God is comprehended and understood through the incarnate Jesus. Martin Luther made this point when he wrote, "We could never grasp the knowledge of the Father's grace and favor except through the Lord Christ. Jesus is a mirror of the fatherly heart [John 14:9; Colossians 1:15; Hebrews 1:3], outside of whom we see nothing but an angry and terrible Judge."[6]

Just as a mirror offers a perfect reflection, Jesus is the perfect reflection of the Father's heart. He is completely aligned with the Father's will and desire, plans and purposes. If you want to know God, then you need not look to the clouds. You need not look within yourself. If you want to know God, then you simply need to know Jesus. He is the perfect mirror image of the Father: "He is the image of the invisible God, the firstborn of all creation" (Colossians 1:15).

Jesus, the mirror of the Father's heart, is the full embodiment of God's grace and favor. He was conceived by the Holy Spirit as God went to work weaving divinity and humanity together within Mary's womb. He was born to a scared, young mother in the out-of-the-way town of Bethlehem. He was a refugee on the run in Egypt with His

---

6   Large Catechism, Part II, paragraph 65.

family as they fled the sword of a tyrannical ruler. He walked the dusty streets of Nazareth, learned Hebrew, ate bread with olive oil, and attended funerals and weddings. Jesus has firsthand knowledge of family and friendships, political oppression and despotic rulers, happiness and celebration, fear and trembling, peace and power, joy and sorrow, life and death. In Christ Jesus, God knows exactly what it is like to be human.

The language we use to describe Jesus emphasizes the nearness of God. The word *incarnation* comes from the Latin word *carnis*. This word translates into "meat" or "flesh" and illustrates the fleshy nature of Jesus. God has joined Himself with flesh in the incarnation (in-*carnis*-ation) of Jesus—a bold confession that God has taken on human flesh and bones, muscle and sinew, blood and plasma, and everything else that constitutes bodily existence. God has drawn so close to this world that He has forever intertwined salvation with sinew, Christ with *carnis*.

Similarly, the word *human* offers us a vivid depiction of the nearness of God. The word *human* comes from the Latin word *humus*. This word translates into "soil" or "dirt" and recounts the humble origins of humanity as it was created out of the dust of the earth. God took some dirt from the ground, exhaled the breath of life into it, and created man (Genesis 2:7). Human bodies, though they are fearfully and wonderfully made, are derived from mere dirt. Christ Jesus—God in human flesh—is therefore the eternal union of Creator and creation, holiness and *humus*, divinity and dust of the earth that is the human body.

The incarnation defies the notion that God is distant. There is nothing abstract about God coming in human flesh to rescue His creation. Flesh and dirt are not unfamiliar concepts that stretch our mind's understanding; rather, flesh and

There is nothing abstract about God coming in human flesh to rescue His creation.

dirt are among the most simplistic and ubiquitous facets of human life. It is hard to get earthier or more tangible than *carnis* and *humus*. Rather than being in the cloud, God has come to us in the most accessible and comprehensible way in Christ Jesus.

And, to be certain, God did not merely descend into creation to wallow in dust. He came to redeem a sin-shackled creation and bring eternal life in the midst of death. God put on human flesh in order to restore human flesh. He descended into the depths of a fallen world in order to lift it up out of the muck and mire of sin. C. S. Lewis offers a vivid image of the incarnation when he writes,

> In the Christian story God descends to re-ascend. He comes down; down from the heights of absolute being into time and space, down into humanity . . . down to the very roots and sea-bed of the Nature He has created. But He goes down to come up again and bring the ruined world up with Him. One has the picture of a strong man stooping lower and lower to get himself underneath some great complicated burden. He must stoop in order to lift, he must almost disappear under the load before he incredibly straightens his back and marches off with the whole mass swaying on his shoulders.[7]

God descended down into a fallen world through the incarnate Christ. God lifted the world up out of sin when He was lifted up onto the cross. God raised the world up as He was raised from death to life on the third day. The profound nearness of God is made known through the incarnation of Jesus Christ. This is a God who does not just live up in the clouds.

---

7   C.S. Lewis, *Miracles* (New York: Macmillan, 1947), 112, 115–17.

THE TANGIBILITY OF GOD

As all Christians believe, God is a Trinity, a union of three persons: the Father, the Son, and the Holy Spirit. While it is true that God the Son—not God the Father or God the Holy Spirit—assumed a human nature, the unity of the divine persons means that we can say that God was incarnate. This discloses a very different kind of God than what most people imagine Him to be.

Lutheran theology is particularly salient on this topic because it developed during a time when the prevailing image of God was an inaccessible judge in the clouds. Luther lived in a world—much like our own—in which people tried to imagine God apart from the incarnation of Jesus Christ. This led him to warn against the spiritual danger of this practice:

> But true Christian theology, as I often warn you, does not present God to us in His majesty, as Moses and other teachings do, but Christ born of the Virgin as our Mediator and High Priest. Therefore when we are embattled against the Law, sin, and death in the presence of God, nothing is more dangerous than to stray into heaven with our idle speculations, there to investigate God in His incomprehensible power, wisdom, and majesty, to ask how He created the world and how He governs it. (LW 26:28–29)

As an alternative to straying into heaven and speculating about God in the clouds, Luther encouraged believers to anchor their image of God in the incarnation of Jesus Christ:

> For as in His own nature God is immense, incomprehensible, and infinite, so to man's nature He is intolerable. Therefore if you want to be safe and out of danger to your conscience and your salvation, put a check on

your speculative spirit. . . . Therefore begin where Christ began—in the Virgin's womb, in the manger, and at His mother's breasts. For this purpose He came down, was born, lived among men, suffered, was crucified, and died, so that in every possible way He might present Himself to our sight. He wanted us to fix the gaze of our hearts upon Himself and thus to prevent us from clambering into heaven and speculating about the Divine Majesty. (LW 26:29)

For many people, God is, as Luther says, "intolerable." They cannot tolerate the very idea of God, whether in the clouds or in the self. Not only do they not believe in God, but they also reject Him. Usually, if you do not believe something exists—say, ghosts or UFOs—you pay them no mind. But many atheists are angry at the God they claim does not exist, expressing bitterness over His harsh morality and condemning Him for allowing all of the suffering in the world. To be sure, as Luther said, apart from Christ, God appears to be "angry and terrible." But His incarnation in Jesus presents God in a completely different light: gracious, forgiving, and saving. Far from looking down from a distance on a world of evil and suffering, God the Son enters it, taking the sins and griefs of the world into Himself.

Far from looking down from a distance on a world of evil and suffering, God the Son enters it, taking the sins and griefs of the world into Himself.

Of course, all Christians believe in the incarnation and in Christ's saving work, but Luther pushes these ideas with a boldness that goes beyond what most other theologians are willing to say (that Jesus is God's Son, that God accepted His Son's sacrifice, generally speaking of "God" and "the Son" as two related but separate beings). Luther, in contrast, emphasizes that the incarnation must change our very conception of God:

> Therefore whenever you consider the doctrine of justification and wonder how or where or in what condition to find a God who justifies or accepts sinners, then you must know that there is no other God than this Man Jesus Christ. Take hold of Him; cling to Him with all your heart, and spurn all speculation about the Divine Majesty; for whoever investigates the majesty of God will be consumed by His glory. . . . We must look at no other God than this incarnate and human God. (LW 26:29)

"There is no other God than this Man Jesus Christ," than this "human God."

WHERE IS GOD TO BE FOUND?

God has drawn very near to us, in a tangible way, in Christ Jesus. Yet, this nearness and tangibility of God did not end with the ascension. Although Jesus has ascended into the clouds, we need not aimlessly search the clouds for Him. He is hidden, yet present, both in the world (as we will discuss in later chapters) and in the Church, where Lutheran theology stresses the nearness of God in Word and Sacrament. In a world that has no idea where God is located, Lutheran theology revels in the presence of God in the Word, the Sacraments, and the Church.

The Word: Lutheran theology has an exceptional awareness of God's active speaking through the external Word. Instead of emphasizing the furtive possibility that God might speak to you through some inner feeling or experience, Lutheran theology clearly locates God's active

Scripture is much more than distant and dusty words spoken by God long ago; Scripture is a direct confrontation and encounter with God in the present moment.

speaking in the Word. The external Word is the locus of God's proclamation. Scripture is much more than distant and dusty words spoken by God long ago; Scripture is a direct confrontation and encounter with God in the present moment. God's speaking is relocated into the present moment in the hearing of God's Word. Luther understood the hearing of God's Word to be an experience in which Christ comes to us:

> When you open the book containing the gospels or hear how Christ comes here or there, or how someone is brought to him, you should therein perceive the sermon or the gospel through which he is coming to you, or you are being brought to him. For the preaching of the gospel is nothing else than Christ coming to us, or we being brought to him. (LW 35:121)

The proclamation of God's Word, though it may seem like nothing more than a Gospel reading or sermon, is actually God speaking into the here and now. It is God descending and speaking in your ear: He speaks the Law, chips away at your sinful heart, and brings you to repentance through the Holy Spirit. In His Word, He heralds the Gospel to you, proclaims salvation in Christ Jesus, and sets you free.

The Sacraments: The nearness of God is intimately experienced in the Sacraments. Many Christian traditions have concluded, however, that the "finite is not capable of the infinite" (*finitum non capax infiniti*). In other words, these Christian traditions maintain that bread and wine cannot possibly contain the presence of God; the infinite God would never locate Himself in such finite elements. Lutheran theology rejects this notion on the basis of Scripture. It is clear throughout Scripture that the infinite God has often located Himself in finite elements. God spoke to Moses from a burning bush and turned simple dirt into holy ground (Exodus 3:1–5). God moved into the tent of meeting for a period of time (Exodus 40:34–35). God so filled the temple that the priests could not even enter it (1 Kings 8:10–11).

Lutheran theology does not claim that the finite has some innate ability to contain the infinite God. It is not as if bushes or bread are inherently capable of containing God. Instead, as the Swedish Lutheran theologian Gustaf Aulén argues,[8] the infinite God has located Himself in the finite. God has willfully descended from His transcendent majesty and located Himself in the finitude of this world. He is present in, with, and under the bread and wine of Holy Communion. The Holy Spirit is delivered through the waters of Holy Baptism. The peace of Christ is fully present in Absolution. The infinite God is near and present (Matthew 28:19–20), ever comforting His people and dwelling among them in and through the Sacraments.

The Church: God is both hidden and located in Word and Sacrament. This means that the church, where Word and Sacrament ministry occurs, is the locus of God's presence in this world. God has not promised to be present on the golf course. God has made no vow to meet you in the radiant beauty of the sunrise or the stillness of the evening sunset. God never claimed that He would be present by means of some inner feeling in your gut. Rather, God has promised to be present in the Word and Sacrament ministry of the church: "For where two or three are gathered in My name, there am I among them" (Matthew 18:20).

Lutheran theology revels in the presence of God that takes place in the ordinary worship of the local congregation. The nearness of God is not a fleeting experience that occurs only when the lights are

---

8   See Gustaf Aulen, *The Faith of the Christian Church,* trans. Eric Wahlstrom and Gr. Everett Arden (Philadelphia: The Muhlenberg Press, 1948), 57.

low, the feeling is right, and the praise band is really in the moment. God does not wait for the smoke machine and background keyboard music before He will arrive in worship. He comes when the Body of Christ gathers together in His name. He floods the sanctuary with His merciful presence as sins are forgiven. He is near in the reading of Scripture and the preaching of the Gospel. He is truly present in what appears to be nothing more than simple bread and wine. The nearness of God that takes place through the Word and Sacrament ministry of a church may appear to be bland, banal, and boring by worldly standards. The church, nevertheless, is holy ground where the infinite God has located Himself here among us.

To be sure, the presence of God can be devastating. The Old Testament records how the people of Israel "trembled" at the presence of God on Mount Sinai, which became a mountain of fire, smoke, and thunder. The people dared not so much as touch the mountain, lest God "break out against them" (Exodus 19:24). An electrical arc from a powerful generator or a burst of radiation from a nuclear reactor can be fatal. But it would be far more dangerous for a sinful, earthly mortal to wander into the presence of the infinite, all-powerful, holy God. In the Old Testament, the people of Israel needed an intermediary, so God gave them one: Moses, through whom He gave them His Word in the Ten Commandments. For us today, God has given us an even greater eternal intermediary: Jesus, who, as both fully human and fully divine, bridges the chasm that separates us from God. So now God's presence is not devastating, but saving.

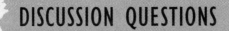

DISCUSSION QUESTIONS

1. What will your faith be like if you believe that God exists only up "in the cloud"?

2. What will your faith be like if you believe that God exists only "inside me"?

3. What will your faith be like if you believe in "this incarnate and human God," Jesus Christ?

4. How would you answer the question "Where can I find God"?

CHAPTER 3

STOP JUSTIFYING YOURSELF

The key teaching of Lutheranism, "The article upon which the church stands or falls,"[1] is justification. The lively marrow of Lutheran theology is justification by grace through faith in the work of Christ. "Justification" has to do with being or being made or being declared "just," or "righteous," or "right." Lutherans teach that we are justified by Christ, who took our sin into Himself and atoned for it on the cross and who imputes to us *His* goodness. When we are united to Christ—which happens by Baptism, in Holy Communion, and when we receive His Word—we are justified, freely, apart from any works of our own. To believe, trust, and depend on the fact that Christ saves us is to be justified by faith. Now, it might seem that justification is another theological term whose meaning has been lost in today's secular climate, for people today do not think they have sins that need forgiving. Christianity, however—in particular, the

---

1   This phrase is often ascribed to Luther, but it is more a summary of what Luther said on the subject. For the origins and history of the phrase, see Alister E. McGrath, *Iustitia Dei: A History of the Christian Doctrine of Justification* (New York: Cambridge University Press, 1998), 448n3.

Lutheran variety—is about the forgiveness of sins. To many others, though, "sin" is thought to be an outmoded concept.

And yet people today still search for "justification" for themselves and what they do. They still crave approval, and they want to consider themselves to be good and right. When they fail to measure up even to their own standards or that of their peers—let alone God's standards—they tend to construct explanations, excuses, and rationalizations that would exonerate them. They try to justify themselves. It turns out that justification is the article on which we all stand or fall.

We can look for justification in moral relativism: "I am a good person, because the moral law I violate does not exist." We can look for justification in our political or ideological beliefs: "I am good, despite my personal failures, because my cause is just." Postmodernism can be a way to justify ourselves: "The truth I reject is nothing more than a construction, so I am blameless in rebelling against it." We can seek justification through atheism: "God does not exist, so no one can condemn me." But these are all simply attempts at self-justification. They are endless mental exercises by which we can consider ourselves to be good. They are attempts to evade the terrifying prospect of God's judgment.

There is an alternative to the hamster wheel of self-justification: "I do not need to justify myself, because the incarnate God justifies me." Once God's Law demolishes our every pretension at self-justification, we can receive the free justification offered by Christ.

THE HUMAN OBSESSION WITH JUSTIFICATION

It has often been said that people today lack a sense of sin. This is because they believe there is no such thing as an objective morality to sin against. They assume morality is purely subjective, a personal code one might construct to give one's life purpose, but it is relative, varying from one culture or from one person to another. No one has the right to "impose" his or her personal morality on anyone else.

And yet, even the most hardened secularists, those who reject the very possibility of moral truth, are constantly making moral judgments: they demand social justice, denounce political evils, demonstrate for human rights, call for ethical approaches to the environment, and criticize bad behavior whenever they see it. Biblical morality, especially when it has to do with sex, seems to carry little weight today, though the outrage at sexual harassment, nonconsensual sex, and other violations shows that sex is still fraught with moral significance. Both social ethics and personal ethics continue to have great force, despite the prevailing worldviews that would seem to give them little basis. God's Law is written on the hearts even of those who do not have God's Word (Romans 2:14–15). It cannot be escaped.

We tend to frame interpersonal conflicts as arguments over moral transgressions—"You're selfish!" "You don't really love me!" "That's not fair!"—with both parties accusing each other and defending themselves. Our transgressions still leave us with guilt, which can torment us for the rest of our lives. And yet we still tend to insist that "I am a good person." If someone else considers us "bad" or "wrong," we defend ourselves—with rationalizations, excuses, and arguments maintaining that our very vices are not bad but good. We do not need to be righteous in order to be self-righteous. If there are no objective moral truths, as so many contemporary thinkers believe, why should any of this matter? But it does.

We soften the demands of God's Law, hoping to evade them. Rather than struggle with God's all-demanding Law, we substitute laws of our own that are easier to fulfill. Instead of worrying about bearing false witness or committing adultery, we recycle, considering

The very evasions of God's Law demonstrate its force.

ourselves righteous because of our environmental sensitivity. With hearts spewing hateful thoughts directed at our neighbors, we consternate over a single plastic cup in the trash. We replace obedience to God with obedience to our peer group. But the very evasions of God's Law demonstrate its force.

The contemporary German theologian Oswald Bayer has shown that, far from being an arcane theological concept, justification is a preoccupation, if not an obsession, for people today.[2] We always feel the need to show that we are right. At work, online, in our casual conversations, in our relationships with others, we are always seeking approval, scoring points, making excuses, and defending ourselves. These are all facets of self-justification.

The word *justify* with its variations is, in fact, a rather common word. "How can you justify spending so much money on a car?" The person being addressed is asked to explain how that purchase was a good thing to do: how was spending so much a "right" decision? Was it a "just" use of resources, or is there something wasteful about it? The question implies a criticism of the person being addressed: in buying the expensive car, were you being selfish, unfair, or foolish—or can you offer an excuse for your action?

Scholars and researchers are asked to justify their work to others in the academy: "How do you justify this methodology in your research?" "What is your justification for excluding this from your argument?" "Will you be able to justify your research practices to the institutional review board?" Academics are constantly engaged in justifying the worthiness and credibility of their work.

---

2   *Living by Faith: Justification and Sanctification* (Grand Rapids, MI: Eerdmans, 2003), ch. 3.

At work, we may hear, "What was your justification for not taking the lowest bid?" Or, "I feel that I am justified in asking for a raise." "What justifies your treating me this way?" "Your justification for being late doesn't hold water." These all involve some sort of accusation or prospect of judgment based on what is just or unjust. And they all appeal to an objective fact as the basis for the justification.

Even when we do not use the word, the desire for justifying ourselves is still present. The comment section of an online article is the modern arena of self-justification. Online discussions consist largely of each commentator trying to show why he or she is right. That usually includes trying to show why others are wrong. Our "rightness" depends on the "wrongness" of others. The currency of this digital self-justification is "likes" and "retweets." Even highly logical arguments are often acts of justification. They frequently fail to persuade others to change their minds because the audience's investment in their own self-justification is impervious to reason.

Just as we are always justifying ourselves, we are also always accusing and judging others. We constantly insist that other people—our spouse, our boss, our government leaders—are wrong, are not doing what they should. Often, such criticism is not dispassionate moral analysis, but rather it is in the context of our self-justification a way of maintaining that we are right because other people are wrong. This is justification by gradation; our flaws are covered by the far greater flaws of those around us.

Just as we are always justifying ourselves, we are also always accusing and judging others.

Our impulse to justify and accuse is the source of our conflicts. "I am right." "No, you are wrong. I am right." "No, you are wrong and I am right." This is the template for broken marriages. The husband and the wife keep accusing each other and defending themselves—bringing up each other's faults, failures, and transgressions; provoking rationalizations and excuses in defense; which, in turn, provoke more disapproval and more justifications—sending the relationship into a death spiral. Social psychologists Carol Tavris and Elliot Aronson, who have written an entire book on the pathologies of self-justification, describe the pattern:

> The vast majority of couples who drift apart do so slowly, over time, in a snowballing pattern of blame and self-justification. Each partner focuses on what the other one is doing wrong, while justifying his or her own preferences, attitudes, and ways of doing things. Each side's intransigence, in turn, makes the other side even more determined not to budge. Before the couple realize it, they have taken polarized positions, each feeling right and righteous. Self-justification will then cause their hearts to harden against the entreaties of empathy. . . . From our standpoint, therefore, misunderstandings, conflicts, personality differences, and even angry quarrels are not the assassins of love; self-justification is.[3]

The same dynamics of back-and-forth accusations and justifications take hold in political debates and when nations go to war. We justify our political party; we justify our country; we justify our ideology. Self-justification also accounts for many of our internal conflicts. Despite all our efforts and what might seem like surface victories, we know, deep down, that we are *not* able to justify ourselves, and our self-accusations create guilt, a sense of failure, and despair. We pat ourselves on the back. We repeatedly say, "I am a good person." And, yet, we know deep down that it is not entirely true.

---

3   Carol Tavris and Elliot Aronson, *Mistakes Were Made (but Not by Me)* (New York: Mariner Books, 2015), 209, 217.

Underlying the need to be justified, Oswald Bayer says, is our yearning for approval, for affirmation, for thinking that our existence matters in some positive way, for our need to think that our life is worthwhile. We keep being accused and condemned, so we continually have to "justify" ourselves, proving that we are right, insisting how good we are, getting defensive, accusing and condemning our critics in retaliation. We want approval. We want to be accepted. We want others to consider us good, even when we are far from good. We rationalize our behavior, "justifying" what we do. This may range from offering a simple excuse to devising a new ethical system, or political ideology, or religion—one that would ratify the way we want to be.

Not only do we judge and justify ourselves and one another; we also judge and justify God. "How can God allow evil and suffering in the world?" both believers and nonbelievers ask. "He must not be good." Against that accusation, believers can form arguments to justify God. Nonbelievers, ironically, justify the intellectual concept of a righteous God by concluding that such a being does not actually exist.

But Bayer shows that the problems of evil and suffering do not go away even when God's existence is rejected. He describes a "secular theodicy." No longer is the question "Why does God allow evil and suffering?" but "Why does existence allow evil and suffering?" If God cannot be justified due to the evil and suffering in the world, existence itself cannot be justified for the same reasons. There is no justification for the physical world. There is no justification for life, nothing to establish its goodness. If existence cannot be justified, life is meaningless, absurd, pointless, and (in a tragic number of cases) not worth living.

But what if, instead of having to justify ourselves, we are justified by *Christ*? What if *God* Himself gives us approval, affirmation, assurance that our existence matters, that our lives are worthwhile? A declaration from God, no less, would settle the question: despite our manifest shortcomings, *He* considers us good; our lives have *His* approval. The incessant desire to earn the approval of others on social media is put to rest when we are justified by Christ.

This entails quitting all of the evasions. Our problem is not just social or psychological. We have to face up to the fact that "I am not a good person." That truth merits not just guilty feelings or social stigma, but God's utter condemnation. But then God's forgiveness means something. The message that Christ has borne the blame comes as astonishing relief, a liberating reprieve.

When we no longer have to justify ourselves, observes Bayer, but know the "passive righteousness" of faith that comes from being justified by Christ, we have the peace that can only come from being justified. We are reconciled to ourselves and do not have to seek our own justification. We are reconciled to God and do not have to justify Him anymore. We are reconciled to others and no longer have to justify ourselves to them. We are reconciled to the world and no longer have to justify our existence. Being justified in Christ Jesus brings peace to our warring hearts.

JUSTIFICATION AND ATONEMENT

How does Christ justify us? By dying.

The Second Person of the Trinity assumed a human nature. He became "the human God." Instead of living in earthly glory, as we might expect and as He was certainly entitled to, He chose to be born in poverty and to live a life of homelessness: "Foxes have holes, and birds of the air have nests, but the Son of Man has nowhere to lay His head" (Matthew 8:20). But He did good works—by His divine power healing the sick, raising the dead, reconciling people who had been at each other's throats—and His teaching blessed the poor in spirit, those who mourn, the persecuted, and so on (Matthew 5:2–11). Jesus' goodness was evident to all, even to His enemies, who hated Him for it. He accomplished what other human beings throughout history have always tried to do but failed: He was justified by His good works.

Jesus' goodness was evident to all, even to His enemies, who hated Him for it.

Nevertheless, He did not escape accusations, judgments, and condemnation. He was, in fact, wrongly convicted and sentenced to death. While others have supposedly died an innocent death, Jesus is the only person to have *truly* died an innocent death. At His execution, though, He fully exerted His divine power by doing something that defies our capacity to understand or to imagine: He took the evils of the world—that is to say, the sins of the entire human race—into Himself. "He Himself bore our sins in His body on the tree" (1 Peter 2:24). St. Paul puts it even more strongly: "For our sake He made Him *to be sin* who knew no sin"— God the Father made Jesus, the sinless one, *to be sin*—"so that in Him we might become the righteousness of God" (2 Corinthians 5:21, emphasis added).

Here St. Paul is also describing what this does for us. Jesus becomes sin so that we can become righteousness. It is not just that we become righteous (adjective); rather, we become righteousness (noun). And we do not just become human righteousness, but we become "the righteousness of God." The Son of God takes our sin and we receive His righteousness. Luther calls this the "wonderful exchange":

> That is the mystery which is rich in divine grace to
> sinners: wherein by a wonderful exchange our sins are
> no longer ours but Christ's and the righteousness of
> Christ not Christ's but ours. He has emptied Himself of

His righteousness that He might clothe us with it, and fill us with it. And He has taken our evils upon Himself that He might deliver us from them . . . in the same manner as He grieved and suffered in our sins, and was confounded, in the same manner we rejoice and glory in His righteousness. (WA 5:608)

When on the cross Christ "bore our sins in His body," He also took the punishment that we deserve. "There is therefore now no condemnation for those who are in Christ Jesus" (Romans 8:1). The "wonderful exchange" also means that Christ's righteousness—along with access to the Father, freedom from guilt, and eternal life—becomes ours. This is like when a couple gets married and each person's assets and liabilities are shared; one person may bring student loan debt into the marriage while the other brings a six-figure retirement savings account. These debts and riches are exchanged when the couple is married. Similarly, we bring sin into our relationship with Jesus, but He brings His goodness, which becomes ours.

God the Father "imputes" our sins to Christ and counts our sins as belonging to Christ. He also "imputes" Christ's righteousness to us and counts it as belonging to us. Thus, when we face the judgment of God the Father, He will consider all of Christ's good works—His healings, His acts of love, His obedience to the Father, His perfect fulfillment of the Law—to be ours. As the Australian theologian John Kleinig puts it, "We therefore know that God the Father is as pleased with us as He is with Jesus, His Son, because we are united with Him."[4] This is what it means to be justified by Christ.

---

4   John Kleinig, *Grace upon Grace: Spirituality for Today* (St. Louis: Concordia, 2008), 52.

BY FAITH

How do we receive this justification? Dr. Kleinig says it happens "because we are united with Him." In the passages we have been discussing, St. Paul says, "*In Him* we might become the righteousness of God." And "There is therefore now no condemnation for those who are in Christ Jesus." We must be "in" Christ, united with Him, somehow connected to Christ on the cross. Faith connects and unifies us with Christ in a veritable marriage of sinner and Savior. Therefore, we are "justified by faith" so that what is ours becomes His and what is His becomes ours. Faith is a gift of God, which we receive by means of the Word and the Sacraments.

> *Faith connects and unifies us with Christ in a veritable marriage of sinner and Savior.*

This is unbelievable, one might think. It would be tremendous if it were true, but how could it be? How could God become a human being? How could anyone—even God—bear another person's sins, let alone the sins of the entire world? It staggers the mind. It is beyond understanding. Interestingly, Luther agrees. "I believe that I cannot by my own reason or strength believe in Jesus Christ, my Lord, or come to Him,"[5] he writes in the Small Catechism, the definitive text that Lutherans use to teach the Christian faith. Essentially, Luther admits, "I believe that I cannot . . . believe."

Notice how Luther is anticipating—and repudiating—the mindset of both the modernist and the postmodernist. "I believe that I cannot by my own reason . . . believe in Jesus Christ, my Lord." So much for the "Age of Reason." So much for modernism. Human reason is not how we receive Christ Jesus and His gifts. "I believe that I cannot by my own . . . strength believe in Jesus Christ, my

---

5   Small Catechism, Creed, Third Article.

Lord." So much for constructivism. So much for the will to power. So much for postmodernism. Exerting our own power or effort is not how we receive Christ Jesus and His gifts. "I can't believe this!" says the modernist. "It's incomprehensible to reason!" "I can't believe this!" says the postmodernist. "I didn't construct this by the strength of my will. This doesn't advance the pursuit of power!" "Right," says Luther to them both. "You can't believe it, not on those terms. Just as I couldn't believe it on my terms."

But then Luther goes on: "But the Holy Spirit has called me by the Gospel, enlightened me with His gifts, sanctified and kept me in the true faith."[6] Faith, this belief and trust in Christ, is a gift from outside ourselves. The Holy Spirit, the Third Person of the Trinity, creates our faith. The true "Enlightenment" is not the "Age of Reason" but the work of the Holy Spirit who "enlightened me with His gifts." Rather than human reason or power, faith is how we receive Christ Jesus. God does this by *calling* me. "The Holy Spirit has called me by the Gospel." To be "called" is to hear a voice, to be personally addressed by words. The Holy Spirit's voice is, by virtue of His divinity, God's Word. Specifically, the call to faith comes from the Gospel, a term that means "Good News."

Faith, this belief and trust in Christ, is a gift from outside ourselves.

Here is how the call to faith happens: First, every pretension at self-justification must be demolished. This is the work of the Law. We have at least an inkling of God's moral law in our conscience, which keeps accusing us as we try to placate it. Society enforces at least some aspects of the moral law. And there are all the demands of everyday life, which may or may not have a moral component, though they all can accuse us and make us feel guilty when we fail.

6   Small Catechism, Creed, Third Article.

But the Bible gives us the true Law, full strength. From the Ten Commandments through the Sermon on the Mount, we have the richest and most sublime accounts of God's moral law. Here are the moral absolutes that define what is right and wrong, the standards that we should fulfill to be "a good person," to be justified. We must emphasize that God's Law—unlike many of its secular substitutes—is good, that it gives the template for justice, mercy, and our own happiness. The problem is, we can never fulfill the Law's demands. We keep falling short of its high standards. The Law, however much we try to follow it, keeps accusing us.

Reading the Bible can be a harrowing experience. Yes, it is magnificent literature. Yes, it is inspiring. But reading about the Law—and the consequences for violating it, namely, God's wrath—can scare us to death. We may conclude that we are "a good person" when judging by our own self-invented standards and grading on a curve. However, we can easily panic when we are confronted with God's standards of goodness. When the Law convinces us that we are not "good" after all, when it knocks down our every attempt at self-justification, we can begin to hear another Word from God: the Gospel.

We hear the Law in Scripture and in sermons. We feel the Law in our conscience. We experience the Law when we get beaten up by life. But the Gospel is the Holy Spirit's Word that rescues us. As we read the Bible, we hear the Law, but we also read about how God keeps rescuing His sinful people; we read about His provision in the temple for sacrifices that cover sins in blood; we read about His forgiveness and His grace. We read foreshadowings and prophecies of a Redeemer—a Suffering Servant, a Prince of Peace, someone who will be called God with us—and then we read the four Gospels that share the accounts of the life, death,

Once we have despaired of justifying ourselves, the message that Christ has justified us becomes our only hope, our salvation.

and resurrection of Christ and the Epistles that explain what all of this means for us. The Law gives way to the Gospel. Once we have despaired of justifying ourselves, the message that Christ has justified us becomes our only hope, our salvation. Broken by the Law, we cling to this Good News, this Gospel, depending on it and reveling in it. This is faith, created by the Holy Spirit through the Word. We are justified by faith.

THE MEANS OF GRACE

The work of the Law and the Gospel in creating faith is not always as dramatic as this description might make it seem. Nor is it a once-in-a-lifetime conversion. Lutherans experience the conviction of the Law—known as "repentance"—and the reception of Christ's forgiveness every Sunday in the Divine Service—in the Scripture readings, the sermon, the corporate confession of sins and the Absolution, and the Sacraments.

The Christian life begins, strictly speaking, with Baptism. The catechism defines Baptism as water "combined with God's word,"[7] so that it conveys the Gospel. We are united with Christ's life, His death, and His resurrection in the waters of Baptism. This includes infants, who, whatever their faults, are incapable of self-justification. In Holy Communion, Christ, by virtue of the Word, gives His actual body and blood "for you," "for the forgiveness of sins."[8] The Sacraments make the Gospel tangible. We will discuss the Sacraments in more detail later, but for now, realize that they are all about Christ's justification.

The point is, we need to continually be brought to repentance by the Law and be brought to faith by the Gospel. As this happens,

---

7   Small Catechism, The Sacrament of Holy Baptism.
8   Small Catechism, The Sacrament of the Altar.

day by day, week by week, through Word and Sacrament, we grow in faith. Which, in turn, bears fruit in good works. The faith that receives Christ's justification works "through love" (Galatians 5:6). Whereupon, God's Law itself takes on a new meaning, becoming a guide for our lives. Christ justifies us; Christ sanctifies us. More on this to come.

OTHER TAKES ON JUSTIFICATION

All Christians believe, in one sense or another, that Christ died for sinners and that we can find justification in His name. But there are important deviations from what we have just described. Catholics, Orthodox, and some Protestants do not believe that Christ's righteousness is imputed to us. Rather, they believe that the forgiveness won on the cross empowers us to actually *be* righteous. This throws us back into the Law and justification by our good works. Evangelicals believe in justification by faith alone, but they tend to understand this as referring to a single time of conversion. After that, we are basically thrown back into the Law so that our good works become central once again. Also, many Evangelicals think of faith in terms of an act of the will, "a decision to accept Christ," rather than the Holy Spirit's work through Law and Gospel.

Calvinists recognize justification by grace through faith pretty much as Lutherans do, but with one major difference: they believe in the doctrine of limited atonement, that Christ died only for the elect. Lutherans believe in universal atonement, that Christ died for the sins of the entire world. As the Bible puts it, "He is the propitiation for our sins, and not for ours only but also for the sins of the whole world" (1 John 2:2). Under Calvinism, one can never be quite sure if Christ died "for me." Christians struggling with that question are encouraged to scrutinize their lives and their inner selves for evidence of "the fruits of faith"; that is, good works. But that, again, throws us back to the Law and good works as the *de facto* basis for the assurance of salvation. Calvinism also creates a system in which *election*—not the cross—is, in effect, the basis for justification.

In contrast, Lutheran pastors assure tormented Christians that Christ indeed died for them. Christians honest enough to admit that inside they are full of sin and death are encouraged not to look at themselves for assurance of salvation but to look *outside* themselves—to the cross, to their Baptism, to Holy Communion, where Christ gives His sacrificed body and sacrificial blood "for you." Lutheran theology emphasizes the *extra nos* (outside of ourselves) nature of salvation: rescue from sin and death comes not from within but outside of ourselves.

Faith is a gift of the Holy Spirit, not a function of our willpower, intellect, or good works.

Yes, Lutherans believe in election, but in a way that removes salvation from the vacillations and uncertainties of human feelings and efforts. Faith is a gift of the Holy Spirit, not a function of our willpower, intellect, or good works. But faith comes to us *objectively* and *reliably* by means of the Word and the Sacraments. To say that Christ died for the sins of the world means, on one level, that the entire world is justified. That is, God declares the entire world "right" or "good." Lutherans call this "objective justification." As we shall see, this doctrine is one reason that Lutherans can embrace the physical realm and secular life so fully. But it is still necessary for individuals to receive this justification that Christ has won for them. This is "subjective justification." Baptism connects individuals in time to the death, burial, and resurrection of Christ (Romans 6:3–5; Colossians 2:11–13). We are also connected to Christ on the cross by means of Holy Communion, in which we are united with Christ through His body and blood (Matthew 26:26–28; Mark 14:22–24; Luke 22:19–20;

1 Corinthians 11:23–25). Through God's Word of Law and Gospel, the Holy Spirit creates faith in our hearts. To be sure, some people have been baptized, have received Holy Communion, and have read God's Word, and yet they have no faith in Christ at all. The Holy Spirit has not created faith in their hearts, at least not yet. Or, rather, they have rejected that faith and are resisting the Holy Spirit. But no one on earth should use the concept of election to conclude that they cannot be saved. Mysteries of that order must await the revelations of eternity.

Some theologians today are attacking the doctrine of justification, along with the related teachings about the atonement. Some insist that these teachings are immoral. It is not just to punish an innocent person—Jesus Christ—in the place of a guilty person—all of humanity. A righteous God, they reason, would not do that. One variation objects primarily to the *violence* of these teachings—the crucifixion, human sacrifice, punishment, and blood. If people think God is this violent, they reason, that would justify (that word again) their own violence! Some feminist theologians say that God the Father pouring out His wrath on His only-begotten Son is "cosmic child abuse." Accusing God Himself of immorality—even in the guise of saying that a righteous God "would not" do such a thing—is a blasphemous role reversal, in which we judge God, rather than God judging us.

Such charges overlook the doctrines of the Trinity and the incarnation. God is not punishing an innocent victim, in the sense of choosing an ordinary mortal to be made a human sacrifice. God is, in effect, sacrificing *Himself*. That God the Father pours out His wrath on God the Son is a cataclysm within the unity of the Godhead. What it means for God the Son to take into Himself all the sins of the world is an unfathomable mystery that only God can do. That He did so to save us puny mortal sinners is a staggering act of grace and love. No, it wasn't "fair" that He had to die to save us. God was not being "just" in justifying us. Rather, He was saving us from justice, giving us what we do not deserve—namely, grace, mercy, and eternal life. This moralistic critique of justification is the ultimate exaltation of the Law, applying it to God the Father and to God the Son in such a way that they fall short. It is a complete rejection of the Gospel, reducing Christianity to just another type of moralism—in this case, to a moralism consisting mainly of pacifism or the condemnation of patriarchy.

For Lutherans, though, the doctrine of justification is the "chief article" on which the Church stands or falls. Justification is the material principle of theology—that is, the substantive content—to which the formal principle, the Word of God, testifies. As we shall see, every other teaching of Lutheranism—the Sacraments, Scripture, worship, vocation, the two kingdoms, prayer, the Christian life—has as its keystone our justification by Christ.

And it is the chief article for a reason. Not only is this the chief article on which the Church stands or falls on justification, but this is also the chief article on which individuals stand or fall. Restless hearts and anxious minds find peace in justification. Frenetic lives of self-justification have rest in the salvation of Jesus Christ. The incessant need to prove our own worthiness and our failure to ever do so are nailed to the cross, buried in the tomb, and put to death forever. Jesus has taken us off the unending treadmill of self-justification and given us unending peace in Him: "And the peace of God, which surpasses all understanding, will guard your hearts and your minds in Christ Jesus" (Philippians 4:7).

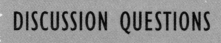

DISCUSSION QUESTIONS

1. How are the contemporary efforts to formulate new moralities an example of the human need to be justified?

2. Give an example of a time when you tried to justify yourself.

3. Explain, in your own words, how Christ justified you by His life, death, and resurrection.

4. Explain, in your own words, how the Holy Spirit creates justifying faith in you by the Law and the Gospel.

5. Some Christians think of the Gospel mainly in terms of their conversion, that moment when they first repented and turned to Christ. What difference does it make for Christians to continually experience the Law and the Gospel, repentance and turning to Christ?

CHAPTER 4

GOD ON A CROSS

One of the most popular varieties of Christianity worldwide is the prosperity gospel. A combination of mainline preacher Norman Vincent Peale's "power of positive thinking" and the Pentecostal Word of Faith Movement, the prosperity gospel represents the theology of most television evangelists.[1] This theology teaches that Jesus died on the cross not so much to atone for sins but to give you your best life now. Faith is not so much trusting Christ to save you but a way of finding health and prosperity. According to the Word of Faith preachers, if you name what you want and claim it in the name of Christ, and if you have enough faith, you will receive it. A new house. A Cadillac. A spouse. A cure for cancer. If you *don't* get it, of course, that means you simply did not have enough faith.

But there is more to this theology. In his prime, Peale was channeling the pop psychology of the 1960s, which taught that our mental states can shape our reality. His disciple, Robert Schuller,

---

1   See Michael Horton, "Evangelicals Should Be Deeply Troubled by Donald Trump's Attempt to Mainstream Heresy," *Washington Post*, January 3, 2017, https://www. washingtonpost.com/news/acts-of-faith/wp/2017/01/03/evangelicals-should-be-deeply-troubled-by-donald-trumps-attempt-to-mainstream-heresy/?utm_term=.75ba35de151c.

with his Crystal Cathedral and television presence, took pop psychology further, teaching a gospel of "self-esteem." He further taught that churches should avoid preaching "negative" ideas, such as sin. He taught the importance of faith, but instead of faith in Christ, he emphasized faith in oneself. If you believe in yourself enough and think positively, you can make your own miracles. For Schuller and pastors he influenced, the Bible was all about principles for successful living. In one book, he turned Christ's Beatitudes into the "Be-Happy-Attitudes." Today, Joel Osteen, television star and pastor of the largest church in America—Houston's Lakewood Church, with 52,000 weekly attendance[2]—is the heir to Schuller with his message of feeling good about yourself. But Osteen works in elements of Word of Faith Pentecostalism. By the same token, faith healers such as Benny Hinn are working in the pop psychology of Peale and Schuller.

The emphasis on the self in this movement is not just psychological but theological, even religious to the point of idolatry. The founder of the Word of Faith Movement, Kenneth Hagin, taught that we are all "little gods." Christians, he said, "are as much the incarnation [of God] as Jesus of Nazareth." "You don't have a God living in you," said Hagin's disciple Kenneth Copeland. "You are one." Today, the popular television evangelist and megachurch pastor Paula White teaches that "Jesus is 'not the only begotten Son of God,' just the first," but now we all are. She has gone on to say that since we are every bit as divine as Jesus, we, too, have the power of the Creator: "There is creative power in your mouth right now. God spoke and created the universe; you have creative power to speak life and death!

---

2   Stoyan Zaimov, "Joel Osteen's Lakewood Church Ranked America's Largest Megachurch With 52,000 Weekly Attendance," *Christian Post*, September 8, 2016, http://www.christianpost.com/news/joel-osteens-lakewood-church-ranked-americas-largest-megachurch-with-52k-in-attendance-169279.

If you believe God, you can create anything in your life."[3]

And what you create, according to these teachers, is wealth, material possessions, and status symbols, what traditional Christians have always condemned as worldly and the trappings of mammon (Matthew 6:24). But White, who once again is so bold as to contradict the Bible itself, has said, "Anyone who tells you to deny yourself is from Satan."[4] Never mind that Jesus Christ said that very thing. ("If anyone would come after Me, let him deny himself and take up his cross and follow Me" [Matthew 16:24].) Despite its Christian trappings, the prosperity gospel constitutes a new religion. In many ways, it is a reversion to animism, which seeks ways to manipulate the gods so they do the will of the devotee. White told her television audience they could "activate" the miracles they wanted by giving money to her ministry, an act that was "going to make God get off His ivory throne."[5]

This is the prosperity gospel. *Lutheranism is not like this*! It may be that Lutheranism is the opposite of this. Luther would call the prosperity gospel an extreme example of a "theology of glory." To this he opposed a "theology of the cross."

He would no doubt have noticed how Paula White repudiated with great blasphemy that biblical text in which Jesus says we must take up our crosses. But for Luther, the cross is not only the basis of our justification, it is also the key to the Christian life, the essence of God's revelation, the way Christianity turns the world—and ourselves—upside down. Luther wrote in capital letters in a commentary on the Psalms, "THE CROSS ALONE IS OUR THEOLOGY."[6]

---

3   These quotations are taken from Horton, "Evangelicals Should Be Deeply Troubled by Donald Trump's Attempt to Mainstream Heresy."

4   Quoted in Horton, "Evangelicals Should Be Deeply Troubled by Donald Trump's Attempt to Mainstream Heresy."

5   Quoted in Horton, "Evangelicals Should Be Deeply Troubled by Donald Trump's Attempt to Mainstream Heresy."

6   Ps 5, 12, *Operationes in Psalmos*, WA 5:176, 32.

This cross-centered theology annihilates both modernism and postmodernism. And it offers a theology of suffering—something sadly lacking in most expressions of contemporary Christianity—that can address our most wrenching troubles. The theology of the cross accounts for our sufferings and the sufferings of God Himself, offering a completely different paradigm for wrestling with the problem of evil.

SELF-WORSHIP

No wonder that the Prosperity Gospel Movement has become so popular today. It accords well with postmodernist assumptions. For all of its associations with the less educated and the poor—people who *need* prosperity, especially its adherents in Latin America and Africa—the prosperity gospel is simply an extreme religious application of the constructivism taught in our sophisticated universities. The self constructs its own reality through its choices and its beliefs. It is only a small step from that truism of the humanities classroom to Paula White's sermon: "You have creative power to speak life and death! If you believe God, you can create anything in your life."

Unlocking the Potential of the Sacred Self

But the same mind-set extends far beyond Pentecostal megachurches and television evangelists. More secularized versions can be found in inspirational seminars, self-help books, and bestsellers in what one would think would be the sober and pragmatic field of business.

This fixation on the self, combined with our unprecedented level of material affluence, results in an expectation and a sense of entitlement that our life should be glorious. If I am not successful or happy, I *should* be. If I am hurting or unsatisfied, something is *wrong.* I *deserve* happiness. I have to do what's right *for me.* These attitudes, often reinforced in marriage counseling, have led to countless divorces and broken families.

There is a modernist side to today's obsession with the self in addition to its postmodernist constructivism. Although many seek to free the god within, others see the self—themselves—through the lens of modernism, with its faith in inevitable progress and in the new nonrevealed religion. Again, the original Deism stressed a transcendent deity who created the universe as a vast machine but cared little for the individual human beings who inhabit it. (Recall Voltaire's analogy about the king's concern for the sailing ship but not the "rats in the vessel.") But today's version is moralistic therapeutic Deism. God is too kindhearted to punish us or interfere with our lives. What we need for our salvation, in the new sense of help with our problems, is not redemption but *therapy.*

Encouraging. Inspiring. Affirming. Supportive. These words describe the ideal greeting card, support group, or self-help book. Individuals possess an innate inner potential. The capacity for success is hidden within everyone, just waiting to be released. However, life can be hard and people need to be encouraged along the way. The tedium of daily life requires a hearty dose of inspiration. What people need is a life coach—a mentor, a pastor, a best-selling guru, or perhaps a spirit guide or even some version of a god—to come alongside them, affirm them in times of indecision, support them through struggles, unlock their inner potential, and see them through to personal victory.

These sentiments are a vestige of modernity. According to the modernist outlook, the future is bright and human capacity is limitless. Standing on the edge of human history, we possess the tools we need for success, particularly now the technological tools. The

Enlightenment was accompanied by humanism, the exaltation of "man as the measure of all things" (they talked that way in those sexist times). Today the cutting-edge ideals have to do with "transhumanism," in which human beings merge with machines. As the capacity of computers continues to increase exponentially, the time will come when computers will attain consciousness and their artificial intelligence will far surpass human intelligence. (Note how the Enlightenment faith that centered around "reason" has evolved from "human reason" to the theoretically unlimited "reason" of machines.)

We will be saved by our technology. Eventually, human beings will be able to download their consciousness into the internet, achieving a unity with all other minds, making it possible to do without our bodies and thus achieve everlasting life. Whereas the divinization of the self, as seen in the constructivist religions, exalts the individual, this technological divinization is collectivist, as individuals merge into oneness, a secularized, high-tech version of the goal of Eastern religions.

The unfettered confidence and optimism of modernity—exponential growth! continual evolution! never-ending progress!—have become features of contemporary spirituality. There is a widespread expectation that the spiritual life should thrive with the right encouragement, inspiration, and knowledge. If we just learn the spiritual principles that are the keys to success and enlightenment and put them into practice, our problems will be no more. But we have to follow those principles, if we can only discover what they are. Everything depends on the self—my choices, my actions, my thinking—rather than on God, who might do our bidding if we follow the right steps but otherwise does not get all that involved.

Ours is a time of rampant self-worship. Although present in every generation, self-worship has found unprecedented success in today's spirituality: nothing is more sacred than the self. Giving glory to the self through the "selfie" is a sacred icon of modern spirituality. Nothing is more valuable than allowing your inner self to flourish through all kinds of self-centered spiritual practices, whether secular or overtly religious: self-esteem, self-expression, self-identify, self-exploration, self-quantification. *Ours is a time* Meditation, positive thinking, and transmigration *of rampant* of the soul are all predicated on awakening some *self-worship.* sort of hidden *gnosis* within everyone. The convoluted world of new age spirituality is a protean mess of beliefs and practices that have little in common with one another. Nevertheless, the one thing they all have in common is seeking to unlock the potential of the sacred self.

Christianity is not immune to this movement. It has been tempted to combine the best of greeting-card sentimentality, support-group encouragement, and self-help inspiration to create the ultimate theology of glory. Many preachers today hope to speak spiritually motivating words that rouse the hearts and minds of listeners so they can live their best lives now. The goal of the sermon is to never offend, always encourage, and leave people juiced up to take on the week ahead. Like a human Pinterest page, the pastor is expected to delight and entertain, inspire and show you what your life can look like if you simply try this out for yourself. Success and victory, health and wealth can all be yours if you just get on board with the program. But there is something seriously missing in this kind of preaching and in the health-and-wealth gospel: Christ crucified.

THE THEOLOGY OF THE CROSS
VS. THE THEOLOGY OF GLORY

In a world fixated on success and glory, Lutheran theology confesses something markedly different: *the best view of reality is from the foot of the cross.*[7] God reveals who He is—and who we are—in the cross of Christ. God comes in suffering and pain to speak the truth. He reveals both Himself and who we are on the cross. This means that the cross is the focal point for understanding both God and ourselves. Rather than fixating on the possibility of success and glory, Lutheran theology asserts that the cross is where the true knowledge of God is located.

Our natural impulse is to desire glory for ourselves—success, acclaim, and victory—and so we look for a religion or theology of glory, one that has answers to all of our questions and solutions to all of our problems, triumphs over all competitors, and exhibits the power of God. And yet, when God came down from heaven, He did so not as a conquering hero or a glorious king; rather, He came as an outcast baby in a manger who grew up to die by the torture of crucifixion. God did not reveal Himself to us in glory but in the cross. To be sure, God is glorious and Christ will come again "in glory," as the Creed says, and in the new heaven and the new earth we, too, will be glorified, finding true success and happiness, of which their worldly counterparts are absurd shadows. But right now, we must give up our glory and our self-made theologies of glory, just as Christ "emptied Himself . . . to the point of death, even death on a cross" (Philippians 2:7–8).

In April of 1518, Martin Luther presented a series of theological

---

7   See Robert Kolb, "Luther on the Theology of the Cross," *Lutheran Quarterly* 16, no. 4 (2002): 464.

statements for debate at the University of Heidelberg. These theses with their brief defenses became known as the Heidelberg Disputation. The theses that Luther presented in Heidelberg offered a different conceptual framework for thinking both about God and the human creature. Luther approached the Christian faith from an angle totally different from that of Scholastic theology. He rejected the notion that human reason, human performance, and human effort could capture God's favor. Instead, he asserted that God reveals the full extent of His love and mercy in the most unexpected way: the death and resurrection of Jesus Christ. Luther proposed a theology of the cross (*theologia crucis*) to replace the predominant theology of glory (*theologia gloriae*).

The Heidelberg Disputation, though it is a profound work consisting of twenty-eight theological statements, is ultimately quite simple. It seeks to cut through all the human constructions of glory, power, and strength and simply let God speak for Himself. Rather than forcing God to conform to human logic, it allows God to tell it like it is: "A theologian of glory calls evil good and good evil. A theologian of the cross calls the things what it actually is" (Thesis 21 [LW 31:40]). Cutting down all the notions of free will, human performance, and seeing through the invisible things of God, Luther sought to anchor theology in the manifest works of God on the cross: "He deserves to be called a theologian, however, who comprehends the visible and manifest things of God seen through suffering and the cross" (Thesis 20 [LW 31:40]).

At the foot of the cross, where both God and humanity are laid bare, salvation is found. Rather than bringing glory to ourselves by trying to win God's favor, the cross is the locus of God's salvation in the world and in our own lives: "The law says 'do this,' and it is never done. Grace says, 'believe in this' and everything is already done" (Thesis 26 [LW 31:41]). Salvation is not obtained through human performance; rather, it is entirely the work of God creating new life amid death: "The love of God does not find, but creates, that which is pleasing to it. The love of man comes into being through that which is pleasing to it" (Thesis 28 [LW 31:41]).

Luther developed his theology of the cross to address the hubris of medieval theology. The renowned Reformation scholar Robert Kolb describes how Luther viewed theologies of glory as being out of touch with reality:

> Luther found these theologies of glory inadequate and insufficient, ineffective and impotent. For such a theology of glory reaches out for a manipulable God, a God who provides support for a human creature who seeks to master life on his or her own, with just a touch of divine help. That matched neither Luther's understanding of God nor his perception of his own humanity. Theologians of glory create a god in their own image and a picture of the human creature after their own longings. Neither corresponds to reality, Luther claimed.[8]

What Luther called the theology of the cross—that sense that we know God most profoundly in weakness and suffering, both our own and that of Jesus Christ—is one of his richest insights. But no one should be surprised that the theologies of glory have been dominant in Church history. Dominance is what the theology of glory is all about: the dominance of reason over theology, the domination of human achievements, the goal of dominating God and making Him do our bidding. Postmodernist critics claim that religion is nothing more than a manifestation of power: the cultural power of privileged groups and the individual's will to personal power. Such a critique is surely unfair and reductionistic, but the theology of glory is indeed

---

8   Kolb, "Luther on the Theology of the Cross," 448.

about power. The theology of the cross, by contrast, with its radical rejection of human power and God's rejection of His own power in His incarnation and crucifixion, is the definitive answer to the post-modernist critiques of Christianity.

The theology of the cross has always been a part of the spiritual lives of Christians who despair of their own works to trust in Christ crucified and who experience tribulation in the world. And yet, as a theological formulation, Luther's way of making the cross founda-tional to all of theology would soon be supplanted by more "glori-ous" approaches to God, even in Protestantism. In place of Christ on the cross, the central principle of Calvinism—in its own words—is "the glory of God." This, ironically, ran parallel to the mind-set of the Counter-Reformation, with the Jesuit slogan, "To the greater glory of God." And certainly, the seventeenth century was an age of glory and an age of power—from the confident splendor of baroque architecture to the struggle for political power between the Catholic absolute monarchs and the new Protestant parliamentary govern-ments—though the Thirty Years' War soon chastened Christendom with the testing of the cross.

Christianity continued to develop theologies of glory such as mil-lennialism, the social gospel, and miracle-expecting Pentecostalism. But the spiritual impulse for glory soon crossed over into the secular-ist arena, where it could flourish free of any constraints of Scripture or incarnation. The Jesuits and Calvinists had already exalted reason, preparing the way for the Enlightenment of the eighteenth century, which rejected revelation altogether in its confidence in reason and reason alone. Just as the Age of Reason ended with the Reign of Terror, later schemes of utopian glory—such as Fascism and Com-munism—ended with the nightmare of unrestrained human sin.

It was precisely in the wreckage of those utopian failures that some theologians rediscovered this teaching of Luther's—the theology of the cross—that had been all but forgotten. Alister McGrath shows how this doctrine arose again in response to what he called "the shattering of liberal Protestant values and aspirations" in the wars of the twentieth century. "Luther's theology of the cross assumed its new significance," says McGrath, "because it was the theology which addressed the question which could not be ignored: is God *really* there, amidst the devastation and dereliction of civilization? Luther's proclamation of the hidden presence of God in the dereliction of Calvary, and of the Christ who was forsaken on the cross, struck a deep chord of sympathy in those who felt themselves abandoned by God, and unable to discern his presence anywhere."[9] Those feelings persist even in the comforts and affluence of our postmodern times.

SUFFERING

Another trait of contemporary culture and spirituality is our assumption that suffering is intrinsically evil and meaningless. Suffering, we think, is to be avoided at all costs. We would rather die—to the point of demanding to be killed by our own doctors—than suffer. We have advanced so far in medicine, technology, and affluence that comfort and pleasure have become some of our highest values. And as we in the twenty-first century West arguably suffer less than any other human beings in history, we consider any kind of pain, be it physical or emotional, to be an aberration, without purpose or meaning.

Of course, human beings have always hated suffering, and rightly so. And yet, Luther in the Heidelberg Disputation, without at all minimizing the horrors of suffering, holds forth an aspect of its value:

---

9   Alister McGrath, *Luther's Theology of the Cross: Martin Luther's Theological Breakthrough* (Cambridge, MA: Blackwell, 1990), 179.

> That person does not deserve to be called a theologian who looks upon the invisible things of God as though they were clearly perceptible in those things which have actually happened. (Thesis 19)

> He deserves to be called a theologian, however, who comprehends the visible and manifest things of God seen through suffering and the cross. (Thesis 20 [LW 31:52])

Gerhard Forde in his commentary on the Heidelberg Disputation,[10] says that the reflex that automatically considers suffering to be evil is part of what Luther is referring to in Thesis 21 when he says, "A theologian of glory calls evil good and good evil," that puzzling statement that we quoted previously. Here is Luther's proof of that thesis:

> This is clear: He who does not know Christ does not know God hidden in suffering. Therefore he prefers works to suffering, glory to the cross, strength to weakness, wisdom to folly, and, in general, good to evil....Thus they call the good of the cross evil and the evil of a deed good. God can be found only in suffering and the cross. (LW 31:53)

Observes McGrath,

> Far from regarding suffering or evil as a nonsensical intrusion into the world (which Luther regards as the opinion of a "theologian of glory"), the "theologian of the cross" regards such suffering as his most precious treasure, for revealed and yet hidden in precisely such sufferings is none other than the living God, working out the salvation of those whom he loves.[11]

---

10 Gerhard Forde, *On Being a Theologian of the Cross: Reflections on Luther's Heidelberg Disputation, 1518* (Grand Rapids, MI: Eerdmans, 1997), 82.

11 Mc Grath, *Luther's Theology of the Cross*, 151.

But in what sense can suffering ever be good? "Evil does cause suffering," says Forde, "but not always."

> However, the causes of suffering may not always be evil—perhaps not even most of the time. Love can cause suffering. Beauty can be the occasion for suffering. Children with their demands and impetuous cries can cause suffering. Just the toil and trouble of daily life can cause suffering, and so on. Yet these are surely not to be termed evil.[12]

The suffering of others can move us to compassion. Our own suffering can force us into greater faith in God. And God's suffering—in the cross of Jesus Christ—gives us salvation.

This point is especially important in light of the chief reason that people today give for refusing to believe in the existence of God. "I cannot believe in a God," they say, "who allows there to be suffering in the world." "A good and all-powerful God," they argue, "would not allow suffering. There is suffering, and so God is either not good, or not all-powerful, or"—their main conclusion—"He does not exist." Christians attempt to answer that argument by constructing so-called theodicies, a term that literally means "justifying God." "It is remarkable," says Forde, "that there were so few attempts to construct theodicies prior to the eighteenth century,"[13] despite the human misery from disease and early death, for which there was no remedy. Although believers from Job through the Church Fathers and beyond have struggled to understand how God and suffering can coexist, only with the Enlightenment and the advent of modernity have people presumed to judge God and accuse Him of unrighteousness for allowing suffering.

---

12   Forde, *On Being a Theologian of the Cross*, 84.

13   Forde, *On Being a Theologian of the Cross*, 84n.

Not only accusations of God but also attempts to explain away suffering and make excuses for God are, according to Forde, manifestations of the theology of glory:

> Works are good and suffering is evil. The God who presides over this enterprise must therefore be excused from all blame for what was termed "evil." The theology of glory ends in a simplistic understanding of God. God, according to philosophers like Plato, is not the cause of all things but only what we might call "good." It is hard to see how such a god could even be involved in the cross.[14]

"But is this prettified God the God of the Bible?" asks Forde. "Is it not quite probable that just these attempts to whitewash God are the cause of unbelief?"[15]

In contrast, says Forde, theologians of the cross "are not driven to simplistic theodicies because with St. Paul they believe that God justifies Himself precisely in the cross and resurrection of Jesus. They know that, dying to the old, the believer lives in Christ and looks forward to being raised with him."[16]

A corollary to the preference for this "prettified God," in contrast to what Flannery O'Connor called "the sweat and the stink of the cross,"[17] is a shift in the purpose of preaching and the mission of the church. Instead of preaching and pastoral care that is evangelical—that is, an application of the cross of Jesus Christ to save sinners—preaching and pastoral care have become therapeutic.

Instead of preaching and pastoral care that is evangelical—that is, an application of the cross of Jesus Christ to save sinners—preaching and pastoral care have become therapeutic.

---

14   Forde, *On Being a Theologian of the Cross*, 12–13.

15   Forde, *On Being a Theologian of the Cross*, 85.

16   Forde, *On Being a Theologian of the Cross*, 13.

17   O'Conner, *The Violent Bear It Away* (New York: Farrar, Straus & Giroux, 1955), 8.

That is, they seek to solve people's problems, make them happier, and alleviate any emotional or mental suffering. "Preachers try to prop up our self-esteem with optimistic blandishments," says Forde. "The church becomes primarily a support group rather than the gathering of the body of Christ where the word of the cross and the resurrection is proclaimed and heard."[18]

"SURELY HE HAS BORNE OUR GRIEFS AND CARRIED OUR SORROWS"

During the Reformation, a controversy broke out between the Lutherans and the Reformed over whether it is appropriate to say that in Christ, "God suffered" or "God died." Zwingli insisted that only the human nature of Christ suffered and died; but God, including Christ's divine nature, cannot suffer and die. Zwingli underscored the doctrine of the "impassibility" of God, the notion influenced by Plato and Aristotle that the Deity is an utterly transcendent, self-contained being who is far above any kind of passion. So just the man Jesus died; the Son of God as the Second Person of the Trinity did not. In fact, Reformed theologians would teach that since the divine cannot be enclosed or contained in anything physical, the Son of God had an existence apart from His incarnation in Jesus.

The Lutherans agreed about the divine and human natures, considered separately in themselves, but replied that the incarnation means that those two natures came together in the person of Jesus Christ. No, God the Father didn't suffer, but God the Son did. He did so by assuming a human nature, which made it possible for Him to suffer and to die. But the divine nature thus experienced those things. Another Lutheran theologian, Martin Chemnitz, in *The Two*

---

18   Forde, *On Being a Theologian of the Cross*, xi.

Natures in Christ,[19] explains it this way: Human beings also have two natures. We have a physical nature and a spiritual nature, a body and a soul. What we experience physically we also experience spiritually. When our body suffers, our soul feels that. This is because we are one person.

It's not that Jesus was only human in His body, with His deity taking the place of his soul. Rather, Jesus, according to Chemnitz, had both a human body and a human soul. But the relationship between those two is a helpful explanatory analogy for the Lutheran doctrine of the communication of attributes. In Christ, the divine and the human natures "communicate" with each other. The transcendent immutable God can thus be said to have suffered and died on the cross.

If only an individual man died on the cross, however good and holy he might have been, that would hardly have helped the rest of us. As Luther explained it,

> If it cannot be said that God died for us, but only a man, we are lost; but if God's death and a dead God lie in the balance, His side goes down and ours goes up like a light and empty scale. Yet He can also readily go up again, or leap out of the scale! But He could not sit on the scale unless He become a man like us, so that it could be called God's dying, God's martyrdom, God's blood, and God's death. For God in His own nature cannot die; but now that God and man are united in one person, it is called God's death when the man dies who is one substance or one person with God. [LW 41:103–4][20]

So we are right to say that God died on the cross. This teaching

---

19 Martin Chemnitz, *The Two Natures in Christ* (St. Louis: Concordia, 2007), 34–35.

20 Quoted in the Solid Declaration of the Formula of Concord, Article VIII, paragraph 44.

of the communication of the attributes—which, as we shall see, has other implications—became a distinctive element of Lutheran Christology. It is enshrined in the Book of Concord,[21] the collection of creeds, catechisms, Confessions, and explanations that define Lutheran theology.

The point for now is that if in Christ God suffers and God dies, that has profound implications for the problem of evil and suffering. The question, as ordinarily framed—If God is all-good and all-powerful, why does He allow evil and suffering in the world? Why doesn't He do something about it?—assumes the transcendent, detached God of Deism. God is thought of as looking down on the evil and suffering of the world, doing nothing. From a Christian perspective, this would be an example of what Luther refers to as the "incomprehensible" and thus "intolerable" God, trying to understand God apart from His self-revelation in Christ.

But if we consider "the incarnate and human God," we find a Deity who enters the human condition, subjecting Himself to evil and suffering, "A man of sorrows and acquainted with grief" (Isaiah 53:3). More than that, He somehow took the evils of the whole world and the suffering of the whole world into Himself on the cross. It is a commonplace of Christian theology that Christ bore our sins. But a key biblical testimony about the atonement, the prophecy of Isaiah, says that He also bore our suffering:

> He was despised and rejected by men,
>   a man of sorrows and acquainted with grief;
> and as one from whom men hide their faces
>   He was despised, and we esteemed Him not.

---

21   Solid Declaration of the Formula of Concord, Article VIII.

Surely He has borne our griefs
    and carried our sorrows;
yet we esteemed Him stricken,
    smitten by God, and afflicted.

But He was pierced for our transgressions;
    He was crushed for our iniquities;
upon Him was the chastisement that brought us peace,
    and with His wounds we are healed. (Isaiah 53:3–5)

"He was pierced for our transgressions" and "crushed for our iniquities." This is the "wonderful exchange" that makes possible our justification. This addresses the problem of evil ("How can a righteous God allow so much evil in the world?"). He neither allows it nor does nothing about it. Rather, He takes it into Himself. Furthermore, according to these texts that are often overlooked, "He has borne our griefs and carried our sorrows." This addresses the problem of suffering ("How can a righteous God allow so much suffering in the world?"). He neither allows it nor does nothing about it. Rather, He takes it into Himself. "With His wounds we are healed," both of our sin and of our suffering, as the death of God incarnate ushers us into an eternal life, in which sin and suffering are no more.

This is not exactly a theodicy of the theology of glory variety that has an answer for everything. Rationalists will still demand to know in what sense one being can "bear" the sins and griefs of the world. The moral objection that it is unjust to punish one man for other people's transgressions is taken away, if one believes that it is not just the man Jesus nor "the human nature" of the Son of God but God who put Himself in the balance. And while using a mere man as a sacrificial victim for the sins of the world could be seen, as some critics put it, as a barbarous act of human sacrifice, it is a far different story if God sacrifices Himself to God. A human being might serve as an arbitrary scapegoat who symbolically represents sin and receives its punishment on behalf of the community. But an omnipotent God who makes Himself a sacrificial victim could actually, literally, assume the world's sufferings and sins—even *become* sin (2 Corinthians 5:21)—so that He could receive His own judgment against sin as a reality.

In speaking this way, we are *not* saying that God the Father suffered for our sins (the heresy of *patripassianism*); nor are we denying the impassibility of the divine nature.[22] God the Son had to become incarnate—that is, take on a human nature—in order to suffer and die. He could not have suffered and died otherwise. The transaction between the persons in the Trinity that took place on the cross, culminating in the Son being forsaken by the Father (Mark 15:34), staggers any human comprehension.

Yes, sin still remains, even though the Son of God atoned for it. Yes, suffering still remains, despite the Son of God bearing our griefs. But they have been dealt with. That we know God only through the cross does not deny His glory, nor the glory that awaits us after death. Here we must struggle against our sins and continually have recourse to the forgiveness that is ours in the cross. And in this life we must bear our own crosses (Luke 9:23). But our sufferings, our crosses, are taken up into His. The significance of the suffering of God incarnate is not simply the resolution of a philosophical and theological puzzle. It has bearing on our own sufferings. That God the Son becomes "a man of sorrows and acquainted with grief" (Isaiah 53:3) and that "He has borne *our* griefs and carried *our* sorrows" (v. 4, emphasis added) means God is "acquainted" with the worst we can

---

22 See the "Catalog of Testimonies," 639, the appendix to the Book of Concord that quotes and records agreement with the Church Fathers on the two natures of Christ and the communication of the attributes, showing that Lutheran Christology is in accord with historical orthodoxy.

go through, He is with us in our anguish, and He helps us through it. Indeed, although the horrors of what we might experience won't go away, suffering can bring us into a deeper dependence and a more intimate relationship with Him. That is, it can increase our faith.

Suffering can bring us into a deeper dependence and a more intimate relationship with Him. That is, it can increase our faith.

In place of an indifferent, inactive deity, the cross discloses a God who enters the darkest places of the human condition and gives Himself to overcome the evil. This is a God who shares our agonies and helps us to bear them. This is a God who loves us. This is a God who is for us.

CONTEMPORARY THEOLOGIES OF GLORY VS. THE CROSS

Modernism is a theology of glory. Reason has all the answers. Science and technology can solve all of our problems. Experts can remake society into a utopia. Progress ensures that life is getting better and better.

Postmodernism is also a theology of glory. Human beings construct their own realities. People choose their own moralities. Culture, the arts, ideas, and laws are nothing more than "masks" for power, with one group oppressing the others until the roles are reversed. History, society, and human life are governed mainly by the will to power, with the will—not the intellect—determining the outcomes.

The theology of the cross—the message that God comes not in power but in weakness to human beings not in their strength but in their weakness—overturns both modernism and postmodernism. It's not just the theology but the experience of the cross: suffering, whether physical or mental or emotional, can make the modernist's confidence in reason and progress seem absurd. Sickness, failure, death—these are not mental or social constructions, but hard, objective realities that the postmodernist cannot escape or explain away. At those moments, when the self with its pretentions is shattered, both modernists and postmodernists can become open to the love of God in Christ crucified.

DISCUSSION QUESTIONS

1. What is wrong with the prosperity gospel? How is it a form of self-worship? What happens to those who have faith in the prosperity gospel if they experience financial ruin, failure, and suffering?

2. Explain the difference between a theology of glory and a theology of the cross.

3. It has been said that contemporary Christianity lacks a theology of suffering. As a result, people think suffering is meaningless. We would rather die than suffer. How can a theology of the cross give us a different perspective on our suffering? How can negative experiences actually strengthen our faith?

4. If there is a loving and all-powerful God, why doesn't He do something about all of the evil and the suffering in the world? How do the doctrines of the incarnation and the atonement address that question?

CHAPTER 5

THE REAL PRESENCE

'm not religious," say many people today, "but I'm very spiritual." In other words, they do not care for religious institutions with all of their doctrines, moral teachings, ceremonies, and other trappings. But they have their own private relationship with the "spiritual realm." They might meditate or even pray; they cultivate experiences of transcendence; they acknowledge some kind of spiritual reality. They might even dabble in some version of Hinduism, which teaches that the physical world is an illusion that we can escape through meditation and yoga, or Buddhism, which teaches a way of detaching ourselves from the physical realm with its distinctions from oneness and its inevitable suffering. Today's spiritual-but-not-religious folks agree with many more traditional mystics and religious people that the spiritual is much more significant than the physical.

Christianity, on the other hand—particularly Lutheran Christianity, which makes a special point of it—is a *physical* religion. It teaches that God created and presides over the physical world. Furthermore, God "became flesh" (John 1:14) in Christ, who physically died and physically rose from death. And we are connected to this physical Christ by the physical water of Baptism and the physical bread and wine of Holy Communion. And when Christ physically returns, we will all experience the resurrection of the body in a physically new creation (Revelation 21:1–7).

Lutheranism is sacramental. Sacraments are "rites that have the command of God, and to which the promise of grace has been added."[1] In this, it is similar to Roman Catholicism and Eastern Orthodoxy and different from most of Protestantism. Yes, Anglicans are sacramental, though they allow a wide range of interpretation as to what the Sacraments are and what they do. Lutherans are highly specific in their "high" view of the Sacraments, which in some ways may be even higher than that of the Catholics.

Lutherans believe that Baptism, defined as simple water "combined with God's word . . . works forgiveness of sins, rescues from death and the devil, and gives eternal salvation to all who believe this."[2] This is because the Holy Spirit is truly present in Baptism, creating justifying faith, even in the hearts of infants. Whereas Catholics believe Baptism removes original sin, with later sins requiring the penitential system of Confession and Absolution, Lutherans believe Baptism covers all sin and its benefits are effectual throughout a person's life. To be sure, a person might lose the faith given in Baptism, and unless that faith is continually fed by God's Word, Holy Communion, and Law and Gospel, it is indeed likely to die. But the convert who returns to the faith is returning to Baptism. In fact, much of the Christian life and many of the observances of the Church—the Invocation, "In the name of the Father and of the Son and of the Holy Spirit," Confession and Absolution, the sign of the

---

1   Apology of the Augsburg Confession, Article XIII (VII), paragraph 3.

2   Small Catechism, The Sacrament of Holy Baptism.

cross, the blessings—are allusions to Baptism, designed to remind the baptized of their redeemed status before God.

Lutherans believe Holy Communion "is the true body and blood of our Lord Jesus Christ under the bread and wine."[3] Catholics believe Holy Communion is a sacrifice offered up to God, to be received by those who have been cleansed of their sins by the sacrament of reconciliation. But Lutherans believe Holy Communion comes from Christ down to us, wherein He gives His body and blood to forgive us. As it says in the catechism, "These words, 'Given and shed for you for the forgiveness of sins,' show us that in the Sacrament forgiveness of sins, life, and salvation are given us through these words."[4] Catholics believe in transubstantiation, that the bread and wine become illusions, that the elements are Christ's body and blood only. Lutherans believe in what they call a "sacramental union," in which Christ's body is united to the bread and His blood is united to the wine.

Both in its sacramental theology and elsewhere, Lutheranism offers a theology of presence. While affirming both the transcendence of God beyond His creation and His indwelling in the hearts of His children, Lutherans also teach that God is present in and through the physical realm. This is true of the Sacraments, and—as we shall see later—the earthly and social realms, in which He is present providentially and in our vocations.

Today, both modernists and postmodernists have problems with the objective physical world. This is ironic because they both often assume that the physical world is all there is. They assume that the physical realm has no meaning, that meaning is a purely human enterprise. Often even religious people today share that assumption, so that the physical realm is something from which to escape into a

3   Small Catechism, The Sacrament of the Altar.
4   Small Catechism, The Sacrament of the Altar.

mode of pure spirituality. Lutheran Christianity, in bringing together the spiritual and the physical, has the potential to heal some of the casualties of both modernity and postmodernity, disclosing both the mystery of salvation for eternal life and the mystery of existence in this world.

DISENCHANTMENT AND REENCHANTMENT

The pioneering sociologist Max Weber described the effect of the modern era as "disenchantment:"

> The fate of our times is characterized by rationalization and intellectualization and, above all, by the "disenchantment of the world." Precisely the ultimate and most sublime values have retreated from public life either into the transcendental realm of mystic life or into the brotherliness of direct and personal human relations.[5]

Weber is saying those "ultimate and most sublime values" can still be found, but they are not in "the world;" that is, in objective physical reality. Rather, they must be found in the nonrational realm of transcendental mysticism or in the private realm of the "personal."

Weber made this statement in a lecture, interestingly titled "Science as a Vocation," that he gave in 1918, near the beginning of the intellectual and artistic movement that would go by the name "modernism." Weber's insight, with the contributions of other thinkers, would manifest itself in the "fact/value distinction," the assumption that only facts are rational, objective, and knowable, while values—such as we have in morality, art, and religion—are nonrational,

---

5   "Science as a Vocation," 20, trans. from Max Weber, "Wissenschaft als Beruf," in *Gesammelte Aufsätze zur Wissenschaftslehre* (Tübingen: J. C. B. Mohr, 1922), 524–55, available online at http://www.wisdom.weizmann.ac.il/~oded/X/WeberScienceVocation.pdf

subjective, and relative. Thus, religious beliefs and doctrines cannot be true in the sense that a scientific discovery or a rational proposition can be true. Rather, according to this worldview, religion is a matter of private values, important perhaps to individuals in giving meaning to their lives, but having nothing to do with the so-called real world.

Weber and most later scholars trace this "disenchantment of the world" with the rise of modern science, which, ever since the Enlightenment, has given naturalistic explanations for physical phenomena that used to require religious explanations. For example, the question "Why does it rain?" was once answered, "Because God made it rain." Now we know that it rains because of the complex interaction of cold fronts, relative humidity, air pressure, and other factors that are the domain of the science of meteorology. To be sure, the early scientists were nearly all Christians who ascribed the laws of nature they were discovering to the laws of God and to His design of His creation. But the Enlightenment of the eighteenth century was an age of reason and came to reject the concept of revelation, constructing a religion based on reason alone: Deism. As we have discussed, this religion posited a deity who created the universe and established its laws, but thereafter allowed the creation to run on its own, like a vast machine. In the nineteenth century, according to this narrative, Darwin discovered that the origins of species—and, by extension, the origins of the world—can be explained in terms of closed naturalistic causes, thus doing away with the need for even a Deistic god. At that point, the physical but disenchanted world began to be seen as the only thing that exists, and science claimed the authority to be the source and arbiter of all truth.

But a disenchanted world is difficult to live in.

A disenchanted world is difficult to live in. A physical realm void of spiritual significance has come to lack any significance whatsoever.

A physical realm void of spiritual significance has come to lack any significance whatsoever. Tangible objects are valuable mainly for the ways we can use them. The natural order, though we can enjoy its beauty, is essentially an automaton, mindlessly following impersonal laws, a machine that we might harness for our own benefit but that has no meaning of its own. To be sure, environmentalists have a higher view of nature, but they tend to see it as fragile and at the mercy of human beings, who thus remain separate and alienated from the world they inhabit.

Our physical bodies are also problematic. Do we "own" our bodies, like other possessions? That would imply we have an existence apart from our bodies—a soul, perhaps?—that is doing the owning. Is our body just a shell for this spiritual nature? If so, what we do with our physical bodies—our sex lives, for example—has little to do with our spiritual lives. Today, it is widely assumed that our nonphysical identities can have a different gender than our physical bodies, which may be changed accordingly. Or *are* we our bodies? We can be preoccupied with our bodies—our looks, our health—and often torment them in an effort to make them conform to a Platonic ideal of beauty or strength. Yet even models, movie stars, and athletes can often be heard saying, "I hate my body!"

Today, the religious, the spiritual-but-not-religious, and even the materialists, who believe the physical realm is all there is, are often alienated from the real, tangible world and from their own bodies. This is only intensified by our information technology, with its virtual realities, virtual identities, and virtual environments. Our "body issues," as they say, are at the root of our other troubles over sex (including the disembodied sex of internet pornography), reproduction (abortion vs. giving birth), and our fear of aging (which we try to reverse with plastic surgery, expensive creams and lotions, and perpetual adolescence). Our implicit theology, say some scholars, is Gnosticism, that heresy of Christianity that denies the physical creation and repudiates the body.[6]

And yet, the outside reality impinges on our consciousness. The strange correlation between our minds and the outside world, which we experience when we study the natural order whether scientifically or experientially, suggests that there may be meaning in the physical world after all. We experience suffering, a reality we cannot understand and that is not a construction of the self we can change by an act of the will. We also experience joy in the world, which is hard to account for if the world is truly meaningless. If the world is really value-free, it is ripe for exploitation and degradation. Today, many people recoil at that, as we see with the environmental movement and various attempts to recover what is natural and unspoiled by modern technology. There are now calls for the "reenchantment of the world," though it is not clear how that can be achieved.[7] We are longing for there to be "something more" to life.

THE FINITE IS CAPABLE OF THE INFINITE

It was not just the scientists who were disenchanting the physical world; many Christians were doing the same thing. Nancy Pearcey has shown how Christians living in the Enlightenment era were in many cases complicit with the project of banishing Christianity from the external world.[8] While the Enlightenment rationalists and

---

6   See Harold Bloom, *The American Religion: The Emergence of The Post-Christian Nation* (New York: Simon & Schuster, 1992). "The American religion," according to Bloom, is and, in some ways, has always been Gnosticism. Search for "Gnosticism" on Amazon.com and notice the many new books that are explicitly advocating the Gnostic religion and worldview.

7   See Morris Berman, *The Reenchantment of the World* (Ithaca, NY: Cornell University Press, 1981).

8   See Nancy Pearcey, *Total Truth: Liberating Christianity from Its Cultural Captivity* (Wheaton, IL: Crossway, 2004), 251–324.

skeptics were attacking religious doctrines and dismissing Christian truth claims as irrational and subjective, the Pietist Movement was also in many cases minimizing doctrine, emphasizing subjective experience, and recasting Christianity as a religion "of the heart." Pietism, which began among Lutherans, became an important Protestant theme and continued among eighteenth-century Wesleyans, nineteenth-century American Revivalists, and twentieth- and twenty-first-century Evangelicals and charismatics.

This banishment of Christianity from the physical world is also evident long before the Enlightenment in the sacramental controversies of the Reformation. For nearly fifteen hundred years, the Church celebrated the Lord's Supper with minimal controversy. To be certain, there were substantial issues surrounding the doctrine and practice of Holy Communion: the apostle Paul addressed issues that had arisen in the Early Church, scholastic theology allowed Aristotelian philosophy to warp the doctrine of the real presence, and the Church in the Middle Ages refused to let laity partake of the communion wine. Nevertheless, for many centuries there were no major watershed issues dividing Christianity on the issue of Holy Communion. But that all changed dramatically in the sixteenth century.

THE REFORMATION

The Reformation ignited a firestorm of controversies regarding Holy Communion. These controversies spread throughout Europe and consumed nearly every country and city where the Reformation had taken hold. Places such as Wittenberg, Strassburg, Zurich, and Basel were epicenters of these fiery debates. These factions and debates raged through Europe from 1524–1526 and resulted in many theological treatises discussing the real presence and Holy Communion. These debates came to a head in 1529 at the Marburg Colloquy.

As the Holy Roman Emperor was arming himself to put down the Reformation by force, it was essential that the various Reformation factions unite. The Protestant prince Philip of Hesse summoned Reformation leaders to Marburg, Germany, to settle the controversies over Holy Communion once and for all. The colloquy—which means "conversation"—turned into a debate between Luther and Ulrich Zwingli, the Swiss reformer who would become a pioneer of Reformed theology. The transcript of the Marburg Colloquy has been preserved, and it reads like a screenplay.[9] First, Luther takes a piece of chalk and writes on a table, "This is My body." When Zwingli gives his rationalistic arguments about figures of speech, how "the flesh availeth not," and how a substance cannot be in two places at the same time, Luther keeps coming back to Matthew 26:26: "This is My body." This bread of Holy Communion *is* the body of Christ. Like Luther, instead of trying to explain it rationally or explain it away, we simply need to take Christ at His word: "This is My body."

But there was no agreement at Marburg. The Lutherans and the Reformed went their separate ways. John Calvin was a twenty-year-old Catholic student when the Marburg Colloquy convened, and though his eucharistic doctrine would be arguably "higher" than Zwingli's, recognizing a "spiritual" presence, he would land on Zwingli's side of the great divide. As a result, most subsequent Protestants would become essentially nonsacramental, denying the real presence of Christ in Holy Communion.

The arguments between the two sides, both at Marburg and in later theological discourses, showed fundamentally different assumptions on a wide range of issues, demonstrating Luther's conclusion at the end of the colloquy: "We are not of the same spirit."[10]

---

9   The transcript of the Marburg Colloquy Walther Kohler's *Das Marburger Religionsgesprach 1529: Versuch einer Rekonstruktion*. Leipzig: Eger & Sievers, 1929.

10   See the very end of the Marburg Colloquy transcript. Luther says this to Martin Bucer, not

Consider, for example, the different understandings of the ascension of Christ. In arguing against the Lutheran teaching that the body and blood of Christ are truly present in the bread and wine of Holy Communion, the Reformed camp insisted that ever since His ascension, Christ's body is in heaven. Since He is no longer physically in the world, Christ's body cannot be on the altars of innumerable churches celebrating Holy Communion. Although God became incarnate once, He is here no longer. Denying the real presence means that God is banished from the physical realm.

In contrast, Lutherans insisted that the ascension makes it *possible* for the body of Christ to be on all of those altars. Christ "ascended far above all the heavens, that He might fill all things" (Ephesians 4:10). Now Christ can "fill all things." He is thus present in the world. Indeed, the world is full of Christ.

Lutheran theology refuses to let human reason reign and rule over God's Word. Instead, Lutheran theology puts human reason in service to God's Word. This is known as a ministerial use of reason rather than a magisterial use of reason. Lutherans explain Christ's presence in the Sacraments in terms of God's omnipresence. Now that the incarnate Son has ascended back into the Godhead, He, like the Father, is omnipresent. "God himself is personally present in all things," wrote Luther (LW 37:63), and is "wholly and entirely in all creatures and in every single individual being, more deeply, more inwardly, more present than the creature is to itself" (LW 37:60).[11] Because of the communication of the attributes—that distinctly Lutheran Christology by which we can say that in Christ, God (the divine nature) suffers (through the human nature)—we can also say that Christ's body (the human nature) is omnipresent (through the

---

to Zwingli, as is often reported.

11 Quoted in Michael Lockwood, *The Unholy Trinity: Martin Luther against the Idol of Me, Myself, and I* (St. Louis: Concordia, 2016), 44.

divine nature). And so His body can be on the altars of myriad congregations every Sunday morning.

But the Reformed reply, "This sounds like pantheism! Or, at the least, panentheism! And if that is all you mean by saying that Christ is present in the bread and wine of Communion—explaining it in terms of God's omnipresence—why can't you say that Christ is equally present in a peanut butter and jelly sandwich?" But Luther had an answer:

> Although he is present in all creatures, and I might find him in stone, in fire, in water, or even in a rope, for he certainly is there, yet he does not wish that I seek him there apart from the Word, and cast myself into the fire or the water, or hang myself on the rope. He is present everywhere, but he does not wish that you grope for him everywhere. Grope rather where the Word is, and there you will lay hold of him in the right way. (LW 36:342)[12]

The Word of God is what creates a sacrament. In Holy Communion, the Words of Institution from the Bible—including Christ's command and His promise—establish not just His presence, but His presence in a saving way. According to the catechism, "These words, 'Given and shed for you for the forgiveness of sins,' show us that in the Sacrament forgiveness of sins, life, and salvation are given us through these words."[13] Then the catechism raises the obvious question: "How can bodily eating and drinking do such great things?"

> Certainly not just eating and drinking do these things, but the words written here: "Given and shed for you for the forgiveness of sins." These words, along with the bodily eating and drinking, are the main thing in the

---

12 See Lockwood's discussion in *The Unholy Trinity*, 143, from which this is quoted.

13 Small Catechism, The Sacrament of the Altar.

> Sacrament. Whoever believes these words has exactly
> what they say: "forgiveness of sins."[14]

Theological disputes about the Sacrament tend to fixate on theories of Christ's presence (or absence). But Lutherans emphasize not only Christ's presence but also what He does when He is present. When Christ says in His Word, as proclaimed by the pastor in his vocation, "This is My body, which is given for you" and "This cup is the new testament in My blood, which is shed for you for the forgiveness of sins" (*LSB*, p. 162), the Gospel becomes tangible. Justification becomes physical, something to touch and to taste. And it becomes personal. Christ is there, and He gives Himself "*for you.*" We receive Christ in faith.

Zwingli and his many followers, who formed many different Protestant traditions, would insist that the Sacrament is merely symbolic of Christ's body and blood. But Calvinists can concede a "spiritual presence," a means of spiritually communing with Christ in heaven. And yet Christ specifically called the Sacrament not His spirit but His body. Nevertheless, Calvin and all the Reformed insist that Christ's body cannot be "locally" present in the physical bread, for two objects cannot occupy the same place at the same time. Besides, the Son of God could not possibly be in the bread and wine of Holy Communion because of the maxim, "The finite cannot contain the infinite." The infinite Second Person of the Trinity cannot confine Himself in such a small space as a tiny piece of bread. And to think that physical objects can somehow contain God or even be a god is out-and-out idolatry!

One would think the Roman Catholic position that the bread and wine are transubstantiated into the body and blood of Christ is the opposite of the Reformed view of the Sacrament. But the doctrine of

---

14   Small Catechism, The Sacrament of the Altar.

transubstantiation also assumes that "the finite cannot contain the infinite." The physical elements of bread and wine are only appearances. They are changed, substantially, so that *only* Christ's body and blood are present in the Sacrament; the physical bread and wine are no longer present. In a sacramental version of Docetism,[15] the bread and wine only seem to exist.

Reformed Christology holds to the principle that the finite cannot contain the infinite even when it comes to the incarnation! The so-called *extra calvinisticum*—"the Calvinist beyond"—teaches that the Second Person of the Trinity was never fully contained in the human body of Jesus, that only part of the Son of God was incarnate, with the rest remaining in heaven. The picture that comes to mind is that of Cinderella's stepsister who could only fit her toe into the glass slipper.

But Lutherans insist that the finite *can* contain the infinite.[16] To think otherwise diminishes the incarnation of the Son of God. And it diminishes the omnipotence of God. Not only that, it also confuses what infinity means. Here is how Luther answered Zwingli's insistence that the Communion host or a human body is too small to enclose the infinite God:

> There is no need to enclose him here, as this spirit dreams, for a body is much, much too wide for the Godhead; it could contain many thousand Godheads. On the other hand, it is also far, far too narrow to contain one Godhead. Nothing is so small but God is still smaller, nothing so large but God is still larger, nothing is so short but God is still shorter, nothing so long but God is

---

15 Docetism, from the Greek word meaning "to seem," is the heresy that taught that Christ, while fully divine, only *appeared* to be a human being.

16 For these debates, see Klaas Zwanepol, "Lutheran and Reformed on the Finite and the Infinite," *Lutheran Quarterly* 25, no. 4 (2011): 414–33.

> still longer, nothing is so broad but God is still broader,
> nothing so narrow but God is still narrower, and so on.
> He is an inexpressible being, above and beyond all that
> can be described or imagined. (LW 37:228)[17]

Lutherans bridled at the Reformed arguments that continually made judgments on what God can or cannot do, what is possible or impossible for the Omnipotent.

As for the charge of idolatry, the Reformed and the Lutherans had quite different definitions. For Luther, as Michael Lockwood has shown, an idol is a god devised by human beings apart from the true God revealed in His Word.[18] Using contemporary terms, an idol is a human construction. We worship, trust, and put our faith in our own mental and volitional constructs, rather than the objective God who was incarnate in Christ and who reveals Himself in Scripture. A statue of Baal is an idol, but so is the made-up deity of a false religion, and so is "covetousness, which is idolatry" (Colossians 3:5). For Luther, sin is a kind of idolatry. Trusting in our good works to save ourselves is a kind of idolatry. As Luther said in his explanation of the First Commandment in the Large Catechism, "Whatever you set your heart on and put your trust in is truly your god."[19]

The Reformed, on the other hand, understood idolatry to be any *physical* representation of a deity. A statue of Baal is an idol, but so is a too-high view of the Lord's Supper. So are crucifixes, crosses, stained glass windows, icons, pictures of Jesus, and other kinds of Christian art. Not all of the Reformed went so far—Calvin allowed for paintings of Jesus as long as they were not in church—but *physicality* is what makes a religious expression an idol.

---

17 Quoted and discussed in Lockwood, *The Unholy Trinity*, 156.

18 Lockwood, *The Unholy Trinity*, 156.

19 Large Catechism, Part I, paragraph 3. That entire section sets forth Luther's understanding of idolatry.

For the Reformed, says Michael Lockwood, "God's transcendence over all created things must be preserved at all costs lest we fall into idolatry."[20] Citing other scholarship, Lockwood describes Reformed theology's "hermeneutic of transcendence," which "drew sharp boundaries between matter and spirit, and stressed to a high degree God's transcendence over all finite earthly things."[21] A hermeneutic is a tool or method used for interpretation. Thus, a hermeneutic of transcendence is interpreting or viewing everything through the lens of God's transcendence. In effect, Reformed theology made the "disenchantment" of the world a religious dogma. Centuries before the Enlightenment, modern science, and twentieth century modernism, post-Lutheran Protestantism had already cleared the ground for today's alienation from physical existence—and perhaps it did so more influentially than any movement that followed.

In contrast, Lutherans emphasize the incarnate "human God," the sacramental union of Christ's body and blood with the bread and wine of the Sacrament, and—as we shall see—other manifestations of God's presence in the world. To be sure, Lutherans believe in God's transcendence. As Lockwood explains,

> Luther's willingness to acknowledge that God has bound himself to created means does not mean he was any less convinced of God's transcendence than the Reformed. Quite the opposite. It was his belief in God's almighty power that led him to assert that if the Creator chooses to join himself to part of his creation, and to unite the infinite with the finite by becoming incarnate, he is able to do so.[22]

---

20 Lockwood, *The Unholy Trinity*, 149.

21 Lockwood, *The Unholy Trinity*, 149.

22 Lockwood, *The Unholy Trinity*, 155.

But Lutherans reject the hermeneutic of transcendence, along with its claim to be biblical.

> From a Lutheran perspective, the hermeneutic of transcendence is an alien imposition on Scripture that results in a one-sided reading of it. It latches on to those parts of Scripture that speak about God's transcendence, but can never fully account for all the "incarnational" elements in Scripture, where the transcendent God makes himself present and available to his people through created things.[23]

THE BIBLE ON GOD'S PRESENCE

In the beginning of Genesis, God's presence in His creation is clear and obvious: "They heard the sound of the LORD God walking in the garden in the cool of the day, and the man and his wife hid themselves from the presence of the LORD God among the trees of the garden" (3:8). Notice here that it is not God who is absent or hiding; rather, it is God's human creatures who are absent and hiding. God then pursues them: "But the LORD God called to the man and said to him, 'Where are you?'" (v. 9). It is not Adam and Eve pursuing an absent God asking where He might be. It is not human creatures searching high and low trying to locate God's presence. It is exactly the opposite. Adam and Eve are absent while God is present. Their sin and rebellion led them to hide from the presence of a holy and perfect God; His goodness and love for them led Him to pursue them and reclaim them at all costs.

This is a foundational text for all of Scripture. It recalls how humanity rebelled against God and fell into sin. While Genesis 1

---

23 Lockwood, *The Unholy Trinity,* 155.

and 2 depict God's perfect creation, Genesis 3 recalls the painful fallout that came when God's human creatures rejected their Creator. They hid from God hoping that some shrubbery could shield them from His presence. God, however, was fully present among them and even made His presence known when He called out to them. This pattern—sinners hiding from the presence of God—repeats again and again throughout Scripture. God is always present among His people and He is always making His presence known. God is always pursuing His rebellious creatures, calling out to them with fatherly love and concern, asking, "Where are you?" While He is present, we are absent and cowering in the guilt of our sin.

God is always present among His people and He is always making His presence known.

As the shrapnel of sin was still sinking into their flesh, God was already at work applying the balm of a Savior: "I will put enmity between you and the woman, and between your offspring and her offspring; He shall bruise your head, and you shall bruise His heel" (Genesis 3:15). This first Gospel promise, the *protoevangelium*, was God promising that He would continue to be present among His creation. God declared that He would be responsible for reclaiming His wayward creation. He would drive a nail into the serpent's plans. He would administer the *coup de grâce* and crush the head of Satan. He would win the day and bring His most cherished possession out of hiding.

And God did exactly as He said. He sought out Abraham and was present among him as He made him a great blessing to many (Genesis 12). He sought out His people while they were in Egypt and was present among them as He led them out of bondage and through the waters to freedom (Exodus 14). His presence ensured deliverance for the people: "The LORD will fight for you, and you have only to be silent" (v. 14). He then led His people into the Promised Land as His presence was known through a pillar of cloud and a pillar of fire. This pattern of God coming to be present among His people persisted at Mount Sinai when God said to Moses, "Behold, I am coming to you in a thick cloud, that the people may hear when I speak with you, and may also believe you forever" (19:9). He fought their fights and comforted their afflictions. He commanded the building of the tabernacle to house a physical object, a work of art—the ark of the covenant—and promised, "There I will meet with you" (25:22). The tabernacle also included a table with "the bread of the Presence" (v. 30). To go to the tabernacle and later to the temple was to go into the presence of God. He spoke through the prophets and filled the temple with His thick and undeniable presence (2 Chronicles 7:1–3). Strolling around in the garden, speaking through the prophets, and securing their salvation, God was present and active among His people.

God's unmistakable presence took many forms in the Old Testament. His presence was known through burning bushes, pillars of fire, and clouds filling the temple. God's presence in the New Testament, however, was even more tangible and unmistakable:

> "She will bear a son, and you shall call His name Jesus, for He will save His people from their sins." All this took place to fulfill what the Lord had spoken by the prophet: "Behold, the virgin shall conceive and bear a son, and they shall call His name Immanuel" (which means, God with us). (Matthew 1:21–23)

God was fully present in the flesh and blood of Jesus Christ. His bodily presence was not a fantasy or chimera; God was fully present as He lived and breathed, ate and drank, slept and woke, spoke and lived with us. Martin Chemnitz described the bodily presence of Jesus: "He was in a certain place, and with normal movements in space He moved from one place to another according to the natural attributes of the human body. Thus He was carried in the womb of His mother until the time had come for Him to be born into the world."[24] God was intimately and bodily present in Christ Jesus. His body was a true human body that was definite and measurable. It had a defined, local, and finite position in space. It was in one place and not another; and we know this from John 11: Jesus had to physically go to Bethany (v. 17) because He was previously not in Bethany (v. 15).

In Christ Jesus, God was with us in a real and bodily way according to the natural attributes of the human body. Nowhere was this more obvious than at the death and resurrection of Jesus. The soldiers felt the full weight of His body as they lifted Him onto the cross. The nails were pounded into real flesh and bones. The gnarled wood of the cross was painted crimson with real blood. Real human heat emanated from His body as God gave Himself as a sacrifice for the sins of the world. The weight of a real body was taken off the cross, placed in the tomb, and physically occupied that space. And, after three lifeless days, He warmed again with human heat and vacated the tomb: "He is not here, for He has risen, as He said. Come, see the place where He lay" (Matthew 28:6).

The ascension of Jesus was also a bodily experience: "The account of Christ's ascension is described with reference to the same thing," observes Chemnitz. "It was not a sudden disappearance, for He was carried on high and taken up with a motion which could be observed. A cloud hid Him from the eyes of the apostles, so that by a visible interval of space He ascended higher and higher from the sight of the apostles."[25] Nevertheless, the ascension was certainly

---

24 Martin Chemnitz, *The Two Natures in Christ* (St. Louis: Concordia, 1971), 426.

25 Chemnitz, *The Two Natures in Christ,* 426.

not the end of His presence among us. Jesus is not imprisoned in heaven. He appeared to the apostle Paul (Acts 9:17; 22:14; 1 Corinthians 15:8) with an unmistakable presence.

While on earth, Jesus promised to continually be with His people when they meet together as His Church. "Where two or three are gathered in My name, there am I among them" (Matthew 18:20). And in His farewell and commission to His disciples before His ascension, He looked ahead to the end of time: "Behold, I am with you always, to the end of the age" (28:20).

God has been present among His people from the very beginning. The unmistakable presence of God began in the garden, extended through human history into the life, death, and resurrection of Jesus, and persisted after the ascension. God has always been present among His people. And, in keeping with the truth of Scripture, the presence of God has never been absent from Lutheran theology.

Holy Communion, in which Jesus is fully present, is proof that God is not distant. When Jesus spoke the Words of Institution—"Take, eat; this is My body. . . . Drink of it, all of you, for this is My blood of the covenant, which is poured out for many for the forgiveness of sins" (Matthew 26:26–28)—He was giving a pledge, sign, and seal of His presence. Jesus promised that He would be bodily present among His people in Holy Communion. The institution of the Lord's Supper did not signal the beginning of a long period of absence in which Jesus would ascend into heaven and leave His followers with only the distant memory of His words. On the contrary, the institution of the Lord's Supper was a promise and pledge by God to be bodily present in an unmistakable way. This presence of God is a powerful antidote to the overwhelming sense of absence in the world today.

ABSENCE AND PRESENCE

Complete digital connectivity has led to a dreadful disconnection with the people and places around us.

Absence abounds in contemporary life. Complete digital connectivity has led to a dreadful disconnection with the people and places around us. Tablets and smartphones, emails and tweets, news and newsfeeds are constantly pulling us away from the here and now. We may be physically present in a space, but we are largely absent all throughout the day. Highways are jammed with people texting their friends when they are supposed to be giving their undivided attention to driving. City sidewalks are bustling with people blasting music through headphones while distractedly staring at their phones. Offices are packed with listless employees scrolling through their newsfeeds rather than digging into the work on hand. Dining rooms at home are often occupied with people who are entirely preoccupied with other thoughts and concerns.

Despite being physically present, we are entirely absent. Our focus, attention, and concerns are often not located in the same room as our bodies. We are here but seldom present. The rare times we find ourselves fully present and engaged occur when we are with someone else who is fully present and engaged with us: a deep conversation with a companion, a challenging discussion about a favorite book, or partaking of a wonderful meal with a loved one. These rare moments have a way of keeping our attention because we have the undivided attention and focus of another person. Her eyes are focused squarely on you. The positioning of her body reveals she is deeply engaged in the moment. Her focused attention suggests that being present here and now is supremely important. In these rare moments, you stop checking your phone, contemplating your schedule, or worrying about what is going on at work. The undivided attention, full focus, and complete presence of another person is powerful.

For many people today, modernist or postmodernist, old or young, God is absent. They perhaps do not realize how their own thinking excludes Him and evades Him. Some people do believe in God, but only as an abstraction, rather than as a close, intimate, concrete reality. Others invoke God to fill in the gaps of their knowledge. This is how some Christians over the years have responded to the progress of scientific discovery. Yes, science has now explained *this*, but God accounts for what we do not yet know. Ironically, both the scientist and the believer may share the assumption that the material realm is divorced from God, so that a material explanation somehow rules out any kind of spiritual significance.

The Lutheran theologian Dietrich Bonhoeffer warned against this "God of the gaps" view in a letter written to Eberhard Bethge. Bonhoeffer wrote, "How wrong it is to use God as a stop-gap for the incompleteness of our knowledge. If in fact the frontiers of knowledge are being pushed further and further back (and that is bound to be the case), then God is being pushed back with them, and is therefore continually in retreat. We are to find God in what we know, not in what we don't know."[26] Bonhoeffer warned against using God as a mere stop-gap for human knowledge and understanding. Rather than being the divine filler to close the gaps in our knowledge, Bonhoeffer called for finding God in what we know and where He has promised to be present.

Finding God in what we know—rather than trying to find God in what we do not know—reveals that He is genuinely present in the world that He has made. The Holy Spirit is genuinely present and active in His Word and in Baptism. Jesus Christ is truly present in the bread and wine of Holy Communion, giving us not only His

26 "Letter to Eberhard Bethge, May 29, 1944," *Letters and Papers from Prison*, ed. Eberhard Bethge, trans. Reginald H. Fuller (New York: Touchstone, 1997), 310–12.

spirit but also His body and blood for the forgiveness of all our sins. God fills His creation with His undivided attention, full focus, and complete presence. He is not absent. God is present in real ways.

Long before the accusation that God only fills the gaps in human knowledge, Lutheran theologian Martin Chemnitz provided a powerful rebuttal: "Now Scripture expressly says that God is not absent or far away but close at hand and present, that He fills heaven and earth with His being, His providence, His power, His creative and preserving ability, and His unique rule."[27] And this is not only a passive, observing presence. Chemnitz says further,

> Christ promises to His church, moreover, not only a mere inactive presence, but rather a presence in which He is active and efficacious, which gives an increase, so that the work of the apostles is not in vain; a presence which defends the ministry against its enemies, which converts the hearers, justifies, sanctifies, governs, and saves them.[28]

Distinguishing different kinds of presence—"in the first place He walked on earth, in the second He appears in heaven in glory, in the third He is present in the Supper with bread and wine, in the fourth He is present in the whole church, and in the fifth He has all creatures present with Him"[29]— Chemnitz insists that Christ's presence is *actual.* We cannot fully "put our faith in a phantom or an imaginary Christ who is not really present with us but is only pictured in our imagination as dwelling in us."[30]

Christ is hidden in the bread and wine. But hiddenness is not the same as absence; rather, it is a mode of presence.

---

27   Chemnitz, *The Two Natures in Christ*, 424.

28   Chemnitz, *The Two Natures in Christ*, 449.

29   Chemnitz, *The Two Natures in Christ*, 448–49.

30   Chemnitz, *The Two Natures in Christ*, 450.

To be sure, God is hidden in the world that He has made. Christ is hidden in the bread and wine. But hiddenness is not the same as absence; rather, it is a mode of presence. Just as a boy hiding in the room is *there*—we just can't see him. The hidden God is revealed only by the Word and can be apprehended only by faith. More on that later.

But What Might a Theology of Presence Do for a Culture of Absence?

In his writing on justification, the contemporary theologian Oswald Bayer said that when we are justified by faith, we are reconciled to God, and we are also reconciled to His creation. This is because, he says, God uses the physical world of His creation—water, bread, wine—to bring to us our justification. We might add other physical elements: ink stamped on paper and bound into a book, sound waves vibrating in the air, the body of the pastor presiding in a building made of stone and steel. However, says Bayer,

> The "new creation" is a return to the world, not a retreat from it. The new creation is a conversion to the world, as a conversion to the Creator, hearing God's voice speaking to us and addressing us through his creatures. Augustine was wrong to say that his voice draws us away from God's creatures into the inner self and then to transcendence. Counteracting Augustine's inwardness in its withdrawal from the world, Luther emphasizes the penetrating this-worldliness of God. God wills to be the Creator by speaking to us only through his creatures.[31]

St. Augustine, for all of his greatness, remained something of a Platonist, something he would share with Zwingli and Calvin. This suggests that the rejection of the religious significance of the world

---

31 *Living by Faith: Justification and Sanctification* (Grand Rapids, MI: Eerdmans, 2003), 28.

in favor of the inner self and transcendence is nothing new after all. It is also the basis of medieval asceticism. As we shall see, Luther's sacramentalism is connected to his critique of monasticism and to his doctrine of vocation.

But we can see the effect of the Gospel as expressed in the Sacraments in Luther's own attitude toward God's creation. As a monk, Luther was an extreme ascetic, rejecting the world and all its ways, but when he discovered the Gospel of God's free grace in Christ, he embraced every facet of God's creation. Bayer discusses Luther's "turn from radical denial of the world to an impressive affirmation of everything that is of the world and nature."[32]

> After Luther was thoroughly convinced, because of his new understanding of Word and Sacrament, that the spiritual is constituted in the form of what was earthly—not only negatively but also positively—the spiritual importance of all things earthly was opened to him in a positive sense as well.[33]

"The spiritual is constituted in the form of what was earthly." That is a succinct statement of Lutheran teaching on Christ, the Sacraments, and—as we shall see—the Christian life.

32 Oswald Bayer, *Martin Luther's Theology: A Contemporary Interpretation* (Grand Rapids, MI: Eerdmans, 2008), 141.

33 Bayer, *Martin Luther's Theology*, 141. The italics are Bayer's.

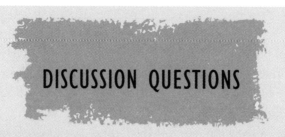

DISCUSSION QUESTIONS

1. How is Christianity a "physical" religion? How does it bring together the physical and spiritual realms?

2. Theology, as well as science, played a role in banishing God from the objective world. This has borne fruit in secularism, the sense that existence is "meaningless," and a new Gnosticism (the view that the physical realm is not important to spirituality). How can a proper recovery of the Sacraments change our appreciation of the physical world?

3. Granted that "God is everywhere," where does the Bible say He is present in special ways? Where is He present "for us"?

CHAPTER 6

THE PURPOSE OF YOUR LIFE

Millennials are said to be entitled, egocentric, and expectant for the world to provide an endless supply of participation trophies. This generation, often defined as individuals born between the early 1980s and the mid 1990s, has been the focus of many recent studies seeking to understand how this subset of the population will transform—and has transformed—the modern workplace. It seems that everyone is trying to understand how millennials think about work.

And it seems that many people are coming up with a peculiar depiction of how this generation makes a living. Millennials are often characterized as compulsively job-hopping, demanding unreasonable workplace luxuries, and needing constant feedback. They supposedly want a workday that begins at 10:00 a.m., offers remote access and ample flextime, fair-trade coffee in the breakroom, and a starting salary close to six figures. "Why should I be limited to the traditional two weeks of vacation time? I want my employer to give me unlimited vacation time." "Technology allows me to be part of a meeting while I am atop a mountain in Nepal; there is no reason why I need to actually be in the office." "I sent an email to my supervisor five minutes ago asking for feedback on my presentation; I suspect her slow response time means she is upset with me." And, as if that is not enough, millennials also want a job that is personally meaningful and fulfilling. To be certain, many of these characterizations are grossly exaggerated and inaccurate caricatures. Nevertheless, some of these *are* accurate depictions of how this generation generally views work.

Despite any supposedly unreasonable requests that millennials make when it comes to work, this generation has accurately diagnosed a serious problem in modern society: the lack of work-life integration. There is a nagging sense that modern life is overly compartmentalized and suffers from a lack of overall integration. Family, work, health, and spirituality are often divided and put in opposition with one another. This causes a great deal of conflict. Spending quality time with your family means not devoting as much time to work. And devoting all your time to work means spending less time with your family. Being healthy and active is quite difficult while tending to heavy workloads and family demands. And a meaningful spirituality is nearly impossible when all your time is spent attending meetings in the board room or taking kids to one activity after another. The millennial generation has raised some important issues for contemporary society by demanding a better work-life integration. They have raised an important question too: how do we bring the disparate pieces of life together into purposeful order?

By asking this question, the millennial generation has unwittingly stumbled on the need to recover the doctrine of vocation. The Reformation contributed three major teachings that would characterize Protestantism in all its diversity: justification by faith, the authority of Scripture, and the doctrine of vocation. The first two still have currency, despite recent criticisms. But the concept of vocation has been gradually lost. First it was turned into a work ethic. Then it turned into a pious attitude empty of specific content. Eventually it was reduced to just another synonym for a job.

Vocation was never meant to be just another word for "occupation." Rather, it was originally about the Christian life that is fully integrated, meaningful, and teeming with purpose. Vocation was the locus for other important teachings, such as the priesthood of all believers, good works, and sanctification. It was not merely a theoretical teaching; rather, as taught in the early Reformation catechisms and sermons, the doctrine of vocation gave practical guidance to Christians in their marriage, parenthood, economic activity, and their role as citizens.

The doctrine of vocation shows Christians how to live out their faith in the world. It is about God's presence in the world and how He works through human beings for His purposes. For Christians, vocation discloses the spirituality of everyday life.

The doctrine of vocation shows Christians how to live out their faith in the world.

Today, Christians are greatly confused about how they should relate to the world. This is evident in the controversies about political involvement and cultural engagement. On the personal scale, champions of "family values" have a soaring divorce rate. Many Christians compartmentalize their lives, conforming to a consumerist and materialistic culture, while pursuing transcendent spiritual experiences that have little to do with their everyday lives. Christians today are variously—and sometimes simultaneously—waging culture wars, withdrawing from the world, and conforming to it.

The time is right to recover the doctrine of vocation. Doing so would revitalize contemporary Christianity and show Christians how they can once again be the world's salt and light.

VOCATION IN THE BIBLE

The word *vocation* is simply the Latinate term for "calling." The best biblical formulation of the concept is found in 1 Corinthians 7:17: "Only let each person lead the life that the Lord has assigned to him, and to which God has called him." Thus, God "assigns" different kinds of "life" for each Christian and then "calls" each Christian to that assignment. The immediate context of that passage has to do with ethnicity (being a circumcised Jew or an uncircumcised Gentile), social position (being a slave or being free), and family status (being married, unmarried, or a widow). These are all "callings."

Elsewhere in Scripture, the apostle Paul has much to say about such callings. In Ephesians 5–6, he explores the relationships of husband and wife, parent and child, and master and servant. Here we find not just moralizing or practical instructions; rather, we are told that God Himself is manifest in these ordinary earthly relationships. Marriage is an image of Christ and the Church. Parenting has to do with God the Father, and, implicitly, God the Son. Servants (or slaves) are serving not so much their masters but Christ. Masters, in their treatment of those who serve them, must remember that they, too, are servants (or slaves) of a Master in heaven. In Romans 13, we are told that all authority comes from God, who gives His authority to human beings in various offices. God works through earthly rulers as His instruments, His agents, to restrain evil and to protect those who do well. Thus, God not only calls and assigns people to different stations in life; He evidently also inhabits them.

Other biblical texts describe God calling people to His service and then giving them specific gifts that enable them to carry out that service. He does this for prophets and for kings—including kings of unbelieving nations—but He also does this for seemingly more mundane kinds of work. For example, He calls the artists who are to make the art of the tabernacle and gives them their talents:

> See, the LORD has called by name Bezalel the son of Uri, son of Hur, of the tribe of Judah; and He has filled him with the Spirit of God, with skill, with intelligence, with knowledge, and with all craftsmanship, to devise artistic designs, to work in gold and silver and bronze, in cutting stones for setting, and in carving wood, for work in every skilled craft. And He has inspired him to teach, both him and Oholiab the son of Ahisamach of the tribe of Dan. He has filled them with skill to do every sort of work done by an engraver or by a designer or by an embroiderer in blue and purple and scarlet yarns and fine twined linen, or by a weaver—by any sort of workman or skilled designer. (Exodus 35:30–35)

And lest we think Bezalel and Oholiab had a unique supernatural giftedness, we are told that God called and gifted other artists, the sign of which was their own desire to create art: "And Moses called Bezalel and Oholiab and every craftsman in whose mind the LORD had put skill, everyone whose heart stirred him up to come to do the work" (36:2). God calls and equips us to serve others in and through our various vocations.

LUTHER ON VOCATION

The great theologian of vocation is Martin Luther. To understand vocation, it is important to start with Luther. Calvin and the Puritans also talked about vocation—and contemporary scholarship about the topic tends to focus on their contributions—but they interpreted God's calling largely in terms of His demands on His followers. This is part of it, but it is essential in grasping the magnitude of this teaching to first understand the sense in which vocation is *God's* work.

Luther emphasized how vocation, like justification, is a function of God's grace. In vocation, God providentially works *through* human beings to care for His creation and to distribute His gifts. The focus is not on our measly efforts or endeavors; the focus is on God using us to accomplish His far greater work through us. This does not just happen occasionally; God is daily and richly blessing His creation by means of our various callings.

> *God is daily and richly blessing His creation by means of our various callings.*

When we pray the Lord's Prayer, to use one of Luther's illustrations, we ask God to give us this day our daily bread. And He does. The *way* He gives us our daily bread is *through* the vocations of farmers, millers, and bakers. We might also add truck drivers, factory workers, bankers, warehouse attendants, and food service workers. Virtually every step of our whole economic system contributes to that seemingly simple bagel you ate for breakfast. And when we thank God for our food before we eat, we are right to do so. He provides our food, and He does so by means of vocation—that is, ordinary people just doing their jobs.

To use another example from Luther, God could have chosen to create new human beings to populate the earth out of the dust, as He did with the first man. But instead, He chose to create new life— which, however commonplace, is no less miraculous—*by means of* mothers and fathers, wives and husbands, in their vocations of the family. God has commissioned us to further His creative work by engendering new life. The words that God spoke in the beginning—"Be fruitful and multiply"—continue to reverberate today through the vocation of mother and father.

God protects us through the vocations of earthly government, as detailed in Romans 13. He proclaims His Word by means of human pastors. He teaches by means of teachers. He creates works of beauty and meaning by means of human artists, whom He has given particular talents. When someone we care about is hospital-ized, we pray for healing. God uses vocation—the work of doctors, nurses, anesthesiologists, and other health-care workers—to deliver that healing.

God's normal way of working in the world is through means. God does not have to use means, and He is capable of working immediately. The word *immediate* derives from Latin (*immediatus*) and shows that there is nothing "in between" or "mediating." God worked immediately when He provided the children of Israel their daily bread—the manna of the wilderness—without farmers and bakers. But God's normal way of operating is through human beings. The infinitely powerful and almighty God of all creation uses plain old people to accomplish His work.

Why? Because He desires us to serve one another.

According to Luther, vocation is a "mask of God."[1] God milks the cows through the vocation of the milkmaid, said Luther. God is hidden in vocation. We see the milkmaid, or the farmer, or the doctor or pastor or artist. We see lab coats, overalls, smocks, and clerical collars. But, looming behind these human masks, God is genuinely present and active in what they do for us. And similarly, as we carry out our various vocations, we, too, are masks of God.

Vocation encour-ages reflection on what God is doing "through" our lives.

Evangelicals often talk about what God is doing "in" their lives. Vocation encourages reflection on what God is doing "through" our lives. Just as God is working through the vocation of others to bless us, He is working through us to bless others. In our vocations, we work side by side with God, as it were, taking part

---

[1] "Exposition of Psalm 147," quoted by Gustaf Wingren, *Luther on Vocation* (Evansville, IN: Ballast Press, 1994), 138. See Wingren also for the other illustrations and concepts from Luther that are cited here.

in His ceaseless creative activity and laboring with Him as He providentially cares for His creation.

THE CHRISTIAN'S MULTIPLE VOCATIONS

Luther taught that Christians have multiple vocations, which, in turn, exist in four estates that God has established to order human life: the Church, the household, the state, and what Luther called "the common order of Christian love."[2]

THE ESTATE OF THE CHURCH

The first calling, or vocation, that every Christian has is to the estate of the Church. Every Christian has been "called" by the words of the Gospel into the life of faith (Romans 8:30), becoming a member of Christ's Body, the Church. In his Small Catechism, Luther says,

> I believe that I cannot by my own reason or strength believe in Jesus Christ, my Lord, or come to Him; but the Holy Spirit *has called* me by the Gospel, enlightened me with His gifts, sanctified and kept me in the true faith.
>
> In the same way *He calls*, gathers, enlightens, and sanctifies the whole Christian church on earth, and keeps it with Jesus Christ in the one true faith.
>
> In this Christian church He daily and richly forgives all my sins and the sins of all believers.[3]

To be sure, God works providentially through nonbelievers as well as believers. Was the farmer who grew the grain for our daily bread or the police officer who kept us from getting robbed a Christian?

---

2   See Luther's "Confession of 1528" in LW 37:365.
3   Small Catechism, Apostles' Creed, Third Article (emphasis added).

Strictly speaking, as far as God's working through human beings, it does not matter. In His governance of His secular realm, God works through believers and nonbelievers equally. But technically, the word *vocation* should probably be reserved for Christians—those who have been "called" by God's Word—with other terms reserved for nonbelievers, such as *stations* or *offices*. At any rate, Christians are those who hear themselves to be personally addressed—that is, "called"—by the Gospel. The Holy Spirit, in Baptism, calls them to faith in Christ and calls them into a community of others who have been similarly called. This, in turn, becomes the foundation for their other callings in the world, the vocations where God assigns them to live out their faith.

God also calls people to tasks and offices in His Church. Pastors speak rightly of being called into the ministry by a congregation, whereupon God works through them to teach His Word, distribute His Sacraments, and give spiritual care to His people. Laypeople, too, are called to do tasks in the local congregation, singing in the choir, serving on committees, serving meals, and in other ways blessing their fellow members. God goes about calling people to tasks and offices in His Church in ordinary ways: a voter's meeting to call a pastor, an invitation to teach a Bible class, a phone call asking for help with sorting inventory in the food bank. The ordinary ways in which these calls occur does not diminish God's work in and through these vocations.

THE ESTATE OF THE HOUSEHOLD

For Luther, the estate of the household includes both the family and the activities by which it supports itself. He had in mind the concept expressed in the Greek word *oikonomia*, the laws of the household. This is the source of the English word *economy*. For Luther, in his day of family-based labor, economic life was connected with family life. Since then, family life and economic life have been split into two realms, and today they are often in conflict with each other. That Luther and the early reformers subordinate economic activity to the family is still significant, however, as modern Christians struggle to order their lives.

Although today we think of vocation primarily in terms of economic activity, Luther has more to say about the vocations of the family. God established marriage, and being a husband or a wife is a vocation. Being a father or a mother is also a vocation. So is being a son or a daughter. So is being a brother or sister, a nephew or uncle, a grandmother or grandfather. One person holds multiple vocations within a family: a woman may be the wife of her husband, the mother of her children, the daughter of her mother, the sister of her brother, and more, with each vocation having its particular dimensions of service.

THE ESTATE OF THE STATE

This estate includes earthly government, but it is also more than that. We might say, the society. Or, better yet, because it is more particular, the culture. This estate involves the many social networks to which we belong. If the household includes the particular economic labor that an individual pursues (as in microeconomics), then the state includes the larger economic inter-relationships (as in macroeconomics). Thus, Luther sometimes discusses particular economic vocations in this category as well.

This third estate recognizes that we were each born into a particular time, place, and society. The cultural context in which we find ourselves is thus part of the life that God assigned us. We thus have responsibilities to our government and to our culture as a whole. Some Christians are called to positions of authority in the government. Americans, as well as many others around the world living in a democracy, have the unusual calling of being both subjects and rulers at the same time, since democratic republics place the governing authorities under the authority of the people who elect them. Christians thus have the vocation of citizenship, which means that politics, civic involvement, and cultural engagement are all realms of Christian service. (Notice how the doctrine of vocation speaks to current controversies about Christians' involvement in politics. The Church can have no political agenda, as such, since the estates are distinct and God operates in each of them in His own way. And yet, Christians do have a vocation as citizens, and they are thus obliged to work for the betterment of the social system in which they find themselves.)

THE COMMON ORDER OF CHRISTIAN LOVE

Our formal positions in the family, the workplace, the church, and the culture are not the only spheres of service to which God assigns us and to which He calls us. Although journalists and others in the news media like to refer to themselves as "the fourth estate," Luther's fourth estate is what he called the "common order of Christian love." This is the realm where people of different vocations interact informally. In Christ's parable of the Good Samaritan (Luke 10:25–37), the priest and the Levite were on the way to serve in their vocations but ignored the man bleeding by the side of the road. In the ordinary course of everyday life and in our relationships with our friends and neighbors, and even with our enemies and strangers, God also calls us to service.

THE IMPORTANCE OF VOCATION IN THE CHRISTIAN LIFE

In stressing the spiritual significance of these ostensibly secular estates, Luther was challenging the Roman Catholic practice of reserving the terms *vocation* and *calling* for religious orders, an individual's calling from God to become a priest, a monk, or a nun. To enter into these "spiritual" offices required taking a vow of celibacy (thereby rejecting marriage and parenthood), poverty (thereby rejecting full participation in the economic life of the workplace), and obedience (which involved substituting the authority of the church for that of the state). Luther countered medieval Catholicism by affirming the very kinds of life that the clerical vows renounced—marriage, parenthood, economic activity, secular citizenship—as being true vocations from God.

Luther's Small Catechism, used for religious instruction for laypeople to this day, includes a Table of Duties, which is described in the headnote as being "Certain passages of Scripture for various holy orders and positions, admonishing them about their duties and responsibilities."[4] The phrase "holy orders," of course, is the terminology for being ordained into the priesthood. But in this section of the catechism that is used to teach the doctrine of vocation, the "holy orders" are not only pastors but also husbands and wives, parents and children, magistrates and subjects, employers and supervisors, and "workers of all kinds."[5]

> Luther insisted that the Christian life requires not withdrawal from the world but rather engagement in the world.

Luther insisted that the Christian life requires not withdrawal from the world but rather engagement in the world. The Christian faith is to be lived out not primarily in the activities of the church—which is the realm of the Gospel, where one receives the forgiveness of sins—but in vocation. Good works belong not so much to the church—to its acts of devotion and its exercises of piety—but to the

---

4   Small Catechism, Table of Duties.
5   Small Catechism, Table of Duties.

world. Our families, the workplace, the country, and the local neighborhood are the arenas in which faith bears fruit in acts of love.

What this meant in practice is that the "spiritual disciplines" moved out of the monastery into secular life. Celibacy became faithfulness in marriage. Poverty became thrift and hard work. Obedience became submission to the law. Most important, prayer, meditation, and worship—while still central to every Christian's vocation in the Church—also moved into the family and the workplace.

Serving God is not strictly confined to "church work" or spiritual exercises. Living the Christian life does not only happen by doing church activities, serving on congregational committees, or mowing the lawn at church. Some Christians are preoccupied with "the Lord's work" while letting their marriages fall apart, ignoring the needs of their children, and otherwise sinning against the actual responsibilities to which God has called them. The doctrine of vocation makes it clear that living the Christian life is not limited to things that happen within the church walls. Rather, the church is the place where Christians come to find the forgiveness of Christ, feed on God's Word, and grow in their faith. Whereupon they are sent out into their vocations—to their spouses, children, jobs, and culture—for that faith to bear fruit.

That the Christian life is to be lived out in vocation is made explicit in the Small Catechism, which also demonstrates how God works through the "calling" that defines the pastoral office. The section on Confession—which Lutherans practice both privately and corporately in the liturgy for the Divine Service—asks, "What sins should we confess?" As we confess our sins, we are invited to think in terms of vocation: "Consider your place in life according to the Ten Commandments: Are you a father, mother, son, daughter, husband, wife, or worker? Have you been disobedient, unfaithful, or lazy? Have you been hot-tempered, rude, or quarrelsome? Have you hurt someone by your words or deeds? Have you stolen, been negligent, wasted anything, or done any harm?"[6]

After this moral scrutiny of the person's various vocations, the sinner confesses those sins to the pastor. At which point, "We receive absolution, that is, forgiveness, from the pastor as from God Himself, not doubting, but firmly believing that by it our sins are forgiven before God in heaven."[7] The pastor, by virtue of his vocation, becomes a channel for God's grace. Yes, only God can forgive sins, but He does so by means of pastors. Just as God supplies daily bread through the vocation of the farmer, He supplies the bread of God's Word through the vocation of the pastor. God Himself is active and present when the pastor proclaims the Gospel of Christ to the penitent sinner.

Thus, in the Order of Confession and Absolution, the pastor asks, "Do you believe that my forgiveness is God's forgiveness?" When the sinner answers, "Yes," thus acknowledging faith in the Gospel and a recognition that Christ is present in the pastor's vocation, absolution is pronounced: "Let it be done for you as you believe. And I, by the command of our Lord Jesus Christ, forgive you your sins, in the name of the Father and of the Son and of the Holy Spirit. Amen. Go in peace."[8] Then the forgiven sinner, built up in his faith through the Gospel, is sent back into his or her vocations to live out that faith.

THE PURPOSE OF VOCATION

But what does it mean to live out faith in one's callings? The Bible is clear: faith bears fruit in love (Galatians 5:6; 1 Timothy 1:5). Here we come to the ethical implications of vocation, and to the relationship between justification by faith and good works. According to the

---

6   Small Catechism, Confession.

7   Small Catechism, Confession.

8   Small Catechism, Confession.

Lutheran doctrine of vocation, the purpose of every vocation is to love and serve our neighbors.

"God does not need our good works," Luther said, "but our neighbor does."[9] Our relationship with God is based completely on *His* work for us in the life, death, and resurrection of Christ. Although we may speak of serving God in our vocations, strictly speaking, we do not serve God. *He always serves us.* Justification by faith completely excludes any kind of dependence on our good works for our salvation. We come before God clothed not in our own works or merits, but solely in the works and merits of Christ, which are imputed to us. But having been justified by faith, God sends us into the world, into our vocations, to love and serve our neighbors, the actual human beings whom God brings into our lives as we carry out our daily callings.

To the monastics who insisted that they were saved, at least in part, by their good works—the prayers, devotions, and acts of piety they do in the cloister—Luther asked, In what sense are these even good works? Who are they helping? Luther criticized monasticism for valuing not only separation from the world, but also—in the cases of some of the most honored monastics, the hermits and the anchoresses—separation from their neighbors. For Luther, good works must not be directed to God; rather, they must be directed to the neighbor, which happens in vocation. Thus is fulfilled "all the Law and the Prophets" (Matthew 22:40), to love God—"not that we have loved God but that He loved us and sent His Son to be the propitiation for our sins" (1 John 4:10); that is, a love that comes from faith—and to love your neighbor, which is the working of faith (Matthew 22:37–40).

---

9 Wingren, *Luther on Vocation*, 10, paraphrasing Luther's *Kirchenpostille*.

Every vocation has its particular neighbors. In the church, pastors are to love and serve the members of their congregation, and the members of the congregation are to love and serve their pastor and one another. The family is a network of mutual love and service. The vocation of marriage entails only one neighbor. Husbands are to love and serve their wives, and wives are to love and serve their husbands. Parents are to love and serve their children, who, in turn, are to love and serve their parents. In the vocations of the state, rulers are to love and serve their subjects. The subjects love and serve their rulers and one another.

In the economic vocations, workers of every kind are to carry out their labors in love and service to their customers. In the simplest terms, a business that does not provide goods or services that people need, or that does not help them in some way, will not stay in business. Vocation, in many ways, replicates the division of labor and the laws of economics. But there is a difference. Free-market capitalism posits each person in the economic order acting in his or her enlightened self-interest—that is, in loving and serving the self. Economics in light of vocation may follow the same laws of supply and demand, competition and markets. However, for the Christian, economic productivity goes far beyond self-interest; rather, it is a way of loving and serving others.

Just as vocation counters the materialism and self-centeredness of economic pursuits by giving them a new meaning and a new orientation, vocation also transforms the nature of authority. Certain vocations do exercise authority over others. Yet this is not just a matter of exercising power over them. Rather, authority must be used in love and service to those under the authority: "You know that those who are considered rulers of the Gentiles lord it over them," said Jesus. "But it shall not be so among you. But whoever would be great among you must be your servant. . . . For even the

Son of Man came not to be served but to serve, and to give His life as a ransom for many" (Mark 10:42–45). Having authority is not a matter of "lording it over" other people, according to Jesus; rather, it is a means of serving them.

Vocation also clarifies moral issues. Parents are called to love and serve their children, not abuse them. Doctors are called to heal their patients, not kill them. The text on the vocation of government leaders, Romans 13, has often been used to quell dissent and to justify absolute obedience to the political status quo. But the leaders, described as agents of God's authority, are charged with punishing evildoers and protecting those who do well. Leaders who do the opposite, who punish the good and protect evildoers, have no calling from God that would authorize such behavior. Leaders are called to love and serve those under their authority and have no warrant from God to exploit and tyrannize them.

Vocations have their authorities, and they also have their authorizations, to the point that some actions are sinful when done outside of vocation but are good works when done within vocation. Luther gave as examples the soldiers' authorization, under a Romans 13 chain of command, to "bear the sword," and the judges' authorization to punish criminals, while the Christian without these callings must forgive his enemies and wrongdoers (see LW 46:87–137). The principle also explains why sex outside of marriage is immoral, but sex within marriage is moral. The difference is not "a piece of paper." It is vocation. We have no calling from God that would authorize having sex with someone to whom we are not married. But within the vocation of marriage, sex is not only authorized, but it also becomes the means by which God creates a one-flesh union, engenders new life, and builds a family.

THE PRIESTHOOD AND ITS SACRIFICES

Vocation has to do with the Lutheran teaching known as the "priesthood of all believers." This teaching does not mean that every Christian is a minister or that ministers are no longer necessary. As we have seen, the doctrine of vocation gives Lutherans a high view of the pastoral office. But notice that Protestant clergy, with the exception of Anglicans, are generally not called priests. Instead, they are ministers, which means *servants*, or, popularly, *preachers*, which focuses on the work of the office. Lutherans prefer the term *pastor*, which means *shepherd*, emphasizing spiritual care. In contrast, a priest is someone who performs a sacrifice. Roman Catholic and Orthodox churches do have priests who are thought to offer up, in the Mass, the sacrifice of Christ. Protestants have always taught that we no longer need sacrifices for our sins, since Christ, our great High Priest, offered Himself as our sacrifice once and for all (Hebrews 9:26). And yet, the New Testament speaks of other kinds of sacrifice and thus other kinds of priesthood. In light of Christ's sacrifice for our sins, God calls us "to present your bodies as a living sacrifice, holy and acceptable to God, which is your spiritual worship" (Romans 12:1).

Loving and serving in vocation involves an act of self-denial for the sake of someone else. That is, it involves a sacrifice. The world is preoccupied with self-assertion and self-fulfillment. Vocation, on the contrary, is about self-sacrifice. That is to say, vocation involves bearing the cross: "If anyone would come after Me, let him *deny himself* and take up his cross *daily* and follow Me" (Luke 9:23, emphasis added). The cross doesn't just signify suffering; the cross is also an instrument of sacrifice. The word *daily* suggests that this passage refers not so much to martyrdom but to the everyday, routine acts of self-denial that take place in vocation. Such self-sacrifice is called for day after day in the Church, the society, the workplace, the family, and the "common order of Christian love."

This spirituality of self-sacrifice for the neighbor illuminates the scriptural passages about different vocations that are so difficult for modern Christians—in our culture of self-assertion, self-actualization, and self-fulfillment—to understand. For example, the Bible instructs wives to submit to their husbands as the Church submits to Christ. At the same time, the Bible also instructs husbands to love their wives "as Christ loved the church and *gave Himself up for her*" (Ephesians 5:25, emphasis added). The husband is not to receive the wife's submission in domination or in "lording it over" her, since that is not how Christ loves the Church. Rather, he is to emulate Christ precisely in "giving himself up" for his wife. Thus, both the wife and the husband are called to sacrifice themselves for each other. Both are presenting themselves as living sacrifices.

The father, coming home from work dead tired, yet still finding the energy to be attentive to his wife and children, has presented his body as a living sacrifice for his family. The mother, yielding her sleep and sanity to the children, has presented her body as a living sacrifice to the family. The same is true for the worker who puts in long hours to do the best job possible for the company's customers. Christ, who is in vocation, takes up all of these sacrifices, small or great, into His sacrifice. And He loves and serves His creation by means of our love and service in our vocations.

To be sure, we often sin in and against vocation. *Instead of serving, we want to be served.* Instead of loving our neighbor, we often use our neighbor for our own selfish purposes. We constantly violate God's design and His calling. As a result, our relationships are often twisted and unhappy, a source of conflict and misery. We must confess our sins against our vocations and against our neighbors

> *Instead of serving, we want to be served.*

and receive the forgiveness of Christ, who bore all of those sins in His body on the cross. And then, in faith, we find love again and work to restore those relationships. This is the Christian life.

VOCATION AND TRANSFIGURATION

The Swedish theologian Einar Billing in his classic work on vocation, *Our Calling*, observes that "In all our religious and ethical life, we are given to an incredible overestimation of the extraordinary at the expense of the ordinary."[10] We expect our religion to give us miracles, spectacular events, and mystical experiences. We often think of morality in terms of major stands on world issues and heroic action. But vocation discloses the spiritual significance of everyday life. Our spiritual and moral lives are to be found in our relationships and in our tasks in our families, the workplace, the Church, and the society. Vocation transfigures our ordinary, mundane existence, charging it with spiritual significance and with the very presence of God.

Luther said that changing a baby's diaper is a holy work (LW 45:39–40). A child doing his chores and a servant girl cleaning the house are outperforming the Carthusian monks in works of holiness.[11] By extension, we can see the office desk, the factory machinery, the computer screen—likewise the voting booth, the marriage bed, the dining room table—as altars on which we exercise our royal priesthood. Luther rhapsodizes on how ordinary tools are sacred means of loving and serving the neighbor:

> If you are a manual laborer, you find that the Bible has been put into your workshop, into your hand, into your heart. It teaches and preaches how you should treat your neighbor. Just look at your tools—at your needle

---

10   Einar Billing, *Our Calling* (Philadelphia: Fortress Press, 1964), 29.
11   Large Catechism, Part I, paragraphs 117–20.

> or thimble, your beer barrel, your goods, your scales or yardstick or measure—and you will read this statement inscribed on them. Everywhere you look, it stares at you. Nothing that you handle every day is so tiny that it does not continually tell you this, if you will only listen. . . . All this is continually crying out to you: "Friend, use me in your relations with your neighbor just as you would want your neighbor to use his property in his relations with you." (LW 21:237)

Vocation changes the quality of what we do. Artists with a sense of vocation will create not just out of self-expression or ambition but also to love and serve—not corrupt or denigrate—their audience. Workers and business executives who see their customers as the objects of Christian love will serve them with their very best work.

From the outside, the economy has to do with the division of labor, individuals pursuing their own self-interests, laws of supply and demand, and other impersonal forces. And so it is, as part of God's created order. From the inside, however, the economy can become transfigured into a vast network of mutual dependence and mutual service, and economic activity can become an expression of love. The daily grind becomes something holy.

Vocation is where sanctification happens, as Christians grow spiritually in faith and in good works. Vocation is where evangelism happens, as Christians teach their children and proclaim the Good News of Jesus to neighbors. Vocation is where cultural influence happens, as Christians take their places and live out their faith in every niche of society.

Vocation is far more than work-life integration, bridging the chasm between personal and professional; it is the integration of heaven and earth, God's work and our work, family and faith, daily life and divine power, culture and the Christian life. Vocation reveals the spirituality of everyday life.

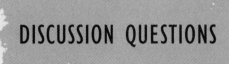

DISCUSSION QUESTIONS

1. God's design for the various estates of human life—including the family, the economy, the nation, the Church, and our informal relationships—is for everyone to love and serve one another. Everyone is to be giving and receiving in a vast network of mutual interdependence and love. But sin interferes. What are the sins and temptations that you must battle in each of your vocations?

2. Name your various vocations in the different estates of your life. How does God work through each of them? Who are the neighbors in each of your vocations whom you are to love and serve?

3. Some Christians associate vocation with self-fulfillment, saying that boring jobs or unhappy marriages are not true callings. What is wrong with that view? How is vocation related to sacrifice? What does it mean to "bear the cross" in vocation?

CHAPTER 7

THE CHURCH AND THE WORLD

Plate tectonics describes the process by which the outermost crust of the earth shifts and slides on the inner mantle. Although the drift of these plates is imperceptibly slow, the friction that arises when they collide is instantly seen by all. The point of convergence and divergence is nothing short of spectacular: catastrophic earthquakes that shake the earth and volcanoes that spew out fiery magma. The movement is gradual; the point of collision is explosive.

Christianity and culture is in many ways like plate tectonics. The convergence and divergence of these two monoliths is imperceptibly slow. It cannot be measured in days or years; rather, it takes multiple generations to see how Christianity and culture shift and slide in relation to each other. However, like plate tectonics, the friction that arises when they collide is evident to all and often explosive. There are numerous friction points today between Christianity and culture: new controversies have broken out over religious liberty, the church's involvement in politics, and the competing claims of church and state regarding moral issues and the institution of marriage. Within the Church itself are contentions over whether Christians should change their worship, their moral teachings, and even their theology to accommodate cultural trends and ideologies. These issues are intensifying as the culture becomes more and more secularized and often hostile to Christian beliefs and practices.

Underlying such frictions is the question of how Christians should relate to the world outside the Church. At one extreme, the World Council of Churches coined a slogan for mainline liberal Protestants: "The world sets the agenda for the Church." At the other extreme are Monastics, the Amish, and other religious communities that insist Christians should withdraw completely from the sinful world. Richard Niebuhr[1] has formulated the options, each of which has Christian adherents: Should Christians separate from the world? Try to rule or transform the world? Or, let the world rule the Church? Or is there a way to affirm and to engage the world without falling into the vice of "worldliness"?

Lutherans have a framework for sorting out these issues that would be helpful for all Christians caught up in these struggles: the doctrine of the two kingdoms. The distinction between God's secular kingdom and His spiritual kingdom—sometimes termed the worldly and the heavenly kingdoms, the temporal and the eternal kingdoms, the kingdom of God's left hand and His right hand—is an important, practical, enormously helpful teaching, but one that is little known and seldom applied today. This is because the doctrine is so widely misunderstood, not only by its critics but also by those who purport to believe it.

The doctrine of the two kingdoms has been construed as teaching separatism (that Christians must remove themselves from the sinful

---

1   H. Richard Niebuhr, *Christ and Culture* (New York: Harper & Row, 1951).

world), dualism (that the Christian life has no connection with life in the world), political quietism (that Christians should uncritically follow even evil rulers), and liberalism (that Christians should uncritically follow all secular trends and ideologies). Properly understood, however, the doctrine of the two kingdoms shows Christians how to live out their faith productively and positively in the secular world. It shows how God is present and active—though hidden—even in the secular realm. Far from being a formula for accepting the political, cultural, or intellectual *status quo*, the doctrine of the two kingdoms offers distinct, specific teachings about these spheres and provides a framework for both a positive and a critical engagement of the secular world.

The doctrine of the two kingdoms shows Christians how to live out their faith productively and positively in the secular world.

MISCONCEPTIONS ABOUT THE DOCTRINE OF THE TWO KINGDOMS

It is important to address the most common misconceptions about this teaching. The Lutheran doctrine of the two kingdoms is often associated with St. Augustine's distinction between the city of God and the city of man. But, not to disparage St. Augustine's insights, the two are quite different in that they are not dealing with the same subject matter. "Two cities," says Augustine, "have been formed by two loves: the earthly by the love of self, even to the contempt of God; the heavenly by the love of God, even to the contempt of self" (*City of God* 14.28). Augustine goes on in his magisterial treatise *The City of God* to explore the conflict between love of self and love of God, using the metaphor of "cities" to address the social implications of these loves. Augustine identifies the city of man with

Rome, which despite its great achievements had recently fallen. The city of God he identifies with the Church. Although Christians, those who love God, must live in the city of man, self-love remains a temptation they must continually overcome. For St. Augustine, the two cities are in an intrinsic conflict with each other.

For Luther, though, both metropolises are located within a larger set of kingdoms whose monarch is God. He is sovereign over both the city of God and the city of man. Luther would agree with the patron of his monastic order that self-love and the love of God are in conflict. This is the problem of sin, which plagues both the secular and the spiritual kingdoms. In fact, in addition to the kingdoms of God, we can speak of the kingdom of the devil, who seeks to undermine and usurp both realms. But the realm of man, however shot through with sin, nevertheless is cared for, sustained, and ruled over by God, who is powerfully present even in the city of man.

Luther applies another kind of love to the secular, temporal kingdom: neither love of God (which belongs to the spiritual kingdom), nor love of self (which can be a symptom of sin), but love of *neighbor*. While the secular kingdom is full of sinners who are, in Luther's terms, curved in on themselves, Christians in their vocations in the world are called to love and serve their neighbors. The worldly kingdom—not the heavenly kingdom, which is all about grace alone—is where good works are to take place, where faith bears fruit in love. In fact, God, who looms behind and works through all of His creation, so orders the world that nonbelievers, the self-serving, and even the wicked, by virtue of their offices and vocations, are compelled to serve their neighbors, even against their will. The social relationships that make up the "city" of human life in God's kingdom of the left is a vast network of giving and receiving, in which everyone serves one another. That is, for all that it is marred by sin, the city of human life, under God's kingdom, is designed to be an embodiment of mutual love.

Seeing the spiritual realm and the earthly realm as being in opposition to each other is to deny God's rule over His whole creation. This manifests itself in separatism, the view that Christians must remove themselves from the sinful world. Thus, in monasticism, fundamentalism, and Anabaptist communitarianism, Christians feel that they must separate themselves completely from the ordinary society in order to live a fully Christian life. The less engagement a person has with the world, the more fully he or she is living the Christian life. Whether this assumption is expressed in monastic vows of celibacy, poverty, and obedience—which repudiate the callings of marriage, parenthood, the economy, and the state—or in Christian subcultures that reject electricity and the automobile, or secular music and other entertainments, such separatism underestimates the scope of God's reign.

Someone else who sees the earthly and the spiritual realms as being utterly incompatible is the dualist, for whom the two have nothing to do with each other. For separatists, the two are, in fact, in relationship with each other, that relationship consisting of opposition and conflict. But for dualists, the earthly and the spiritual realms have no relationship at all. What one does physically has nothing to do with one's spiritual state. By the same token, one's spiritual state has no bearing on one's physical life. Examples of dualists would be the Gnostics who believe that their fleshly life, including their sexual practices, is irrelevant to their spiritual lives; the Deists who believe that God does not intervene in the world or in human lives; nominal Christians who insist that they believe in Christ, though they never go to church or allow their religious beliefs to affect their behavior; millennials and others who are "spiritual but not religious," embracing a completely secularist life and worldview while occasionally practicing religious meditation or prayer.

The doctrine of the two kingdoms, far from being a dualistic separation of the physical and the spiritual, is actually a model for bringing them together and relating them to each other. Both realms have the same King. That there are different kinds of existence we experience is self-evident. But, in the words of the Nicene Creed, the one God is "the maker of heaven and earth and of all things visible and invisible." These are different categories, and their Creator governs them in different ways. But they are all the work of "the Father Almighty."

The doctrine of the two kingdoms joins what is usually separated and *overcomes* dualism, disclosing God's intimate involvement even in what appears to be secular, nonspiritual, and mundane.

Perhaps the most serious misconception about the doctrine of the two kingdoms is that it gives divine sanction to the *status quo*. Because God rules the created and the social orders, including earthly governments, so the reasoning goes, they must be in accord with His will and therefore human beings should accept them. This could mean becoming so conservative that we resist social change and accept every ruler, no matter how oppressive and corrupt, as God's representative (political quietism). Or becoming so liberal that we accept every social trend, cultural shift, and secular ideology as "new things God is doing" (liberalism).

Thus the doctrine of two kingdoms is often blamed for the political passivity of twentieth century German Lutherans. Many say this doctrine not only allowed Hitler to come to power but also led many individuals to fanatical support of the Nazi regime. Actually, the so-called German Christian Movement, which took over the state church, came not from a politically quietist conservatism but from a theological liberalism that rejected the Bible as a "Jewish document;" sought to modernize churches through the thought of Darwin,

Nietzsche, and the "race scientists;" and cultivated a social gospel based on Nazi ideology.[2]

Far from being a period of political quietism and passive acceptance of authority, the Reformation provoked political upheaval, rebellion, and a thorough-going questioning of authority. Luther defied both the pope and emperor. Peasants revolted. Local princes, convinced of the truth of Lutheranism, rebelled against their feudal overlords and, specifically, the emperor. This escalated into armed conflict between the Lutheran princes and the Holy Roman Empire, first with the Smalcald War and, later, the Thirty Years' War. Yes, Luther piously counseled submission, to the point of recommending that the princes turn him over to the emperor to be killed. Yes, Luther urged the princes to quell the peasant rebellion, which had degenerated into bloody anarchy. But Luther never held back from criticizing earthly authorities, from King Henry VIII to some of his own allies among the German princes. The doctrine of two kingdoms does not prohibit Christians from speaking out against princes in the sixteenth century, Nazis in the twentieth century, or the earthly authorities of today.

God is hidden in the world, where He reigns over all things. But at the same time, as Luther says in "A Mighty Fortress Is Our God," Satan is "this world's prince" (*LSB* 656:3). Thus, the world is a battleground between Satan and God, a realm of continual conflict, which is the context for Christians living out their faith in the world. This is not a conflict between the two kingdoms; rather, it is a conflict within the kingdoms. Christians participate in this conflict as they battle sin, struggle against temptations, and undergo trials and tribulations. As they do so—in both kingdoms—they are forced to

---

2   See Gene Edward Veith, *Modern Fascism: The Threat to the Judeo-Christian Worldview* (St. Louis: Concordia, 1993).

depend more and more on God and so grow in their faith.

When we ask God to "lead us not into temptation," says Luther in the Small Catechism, we pray "that God would guard and keep us so that the devil, the world, and our sinful nature may not deceive us or mislead us into false belief, despair, and other great shame and vice."[3] This is a far cry from any kind of complacency or uncritical acceptance of the world.

The implications of the doctrine of the two kingdoms for civil government are set forth with clarity and nuance in Article XVI of the Augsburg Confession:

> Our churches teach that lawful civil regulations are good works of God. They teach that it is right for Christians to hold political office, to serve as judges, to judge matters by imperial laws and other existing laws, to impose just punishments, to engage in just wars, to serve as soldiers, to make legal contracts, to hold property, to take oaths when required by the magistrates, for a man to marry a wife, or a woman to be given in marriage [Romans 13; 1 Corinthians 7:2].
>
> Our churches condemn the Anabaptists who forbid these political offices to Christians. They also condemn those who do not locate evangelical perfection in the fear of God and in faith, but place it in forsaking political offices. For the Gospel teaches an eternal righteousness of the heart (Romans 10:10). At the same time, it does not require the destruction of the civil state or the family. The Gospel very much requires that they be preserved as God's ordinances and that love be practiced in such ordinances. Therefore, it is necessary for Christians to

---

3   The Lord's Prayer, Sixth Petition.

> be obedient to their rulers and laws. The only exception
> is when they are commanded to sin. Then they ought to
> obey God rather than men (Acts 5:29).

Here, civil ordinances are described as "good works of God." These He accomplishes through human vocations, so that Christians may serve their neighbors in civic offices—as officials, judges, or soldiers—and in the ordinary course of their citizenship, owning property, entering into contracts, testifying in court. Marriage is also a civil institution, an important part of God's earthly kingdom, so Christians may marry. The Augsburg Confession here, condemning both the Anabaptists and the monastics, concludes that the Gospel "does not require the destruction of the civil state or the family," but upholds them as God's ordinances where "love" is practiced. Thus, Christians should obey their magistrates and the civil laws, with an important limitation, "The only exception is when they are commanded to sin. Then they ought to obey God rather than men," citing Acts 5:29.

Thinking about the secular realm in terms of the doctrine of the two kingdoms allows for Christians to embrace their lives in the world in all of its secularity because God reigns here too. At the same time, this doctrine gives a framework for battling sin in the world and for critiquing cultures, ideologies, and practices that would undermine God's rule. This framework grows out of three ways that God presides over His temporal kingdom; namely, His Law, His creation, and vocation.

Thinking about the secular realm in terms of the doctrine of the two kingdoms allows for Christians to embrace their lives in the world in all of its secularity because God reigns here too.

THE TEMPORAL KINGDOM AND THE LAW

According to the doctrine of the two kingdoms, God governs His temporal, earthly kingdom by means of His Law. The moral law applies specifically to the secular realm. It does *not* apply, strictly speaking, to the spiritual kingdom. God's heavenly kingdom comes not from the Law but from the Gospel, being governed only by God's grace in the Gospel of forgiveness through the cross of Jesus Christ.

Today, it is commonly assumed that morality is to be categorized with religion. Christians who protest abortion, for example, are often dismissed with the words, "They don't have the right to impose their religious beliefs on anyone else." But opposing abortion is not a religious belief, as such. The essence of the Christian religion is the Gospel, which is not about morality but, rather, is about forgiveness for failing to be moral. Christians do believe in God's Law and use the Law for the conviction of sin and as a guide to life, but the spiritual kingdom—the realm of faith in Christ—is a realm of freedom from the Law. In their life in the world, Christians see the killing of unborn children as an act of monumental cruelty and injustice. But Christianity, as such, is about showing a woman who has had an abortion how to be forgiven.

In their life in the world, Christians see the killing of unborn children as an act of monumental cruelty and injustice. But Christianity, as such, is about showing a woman who has had an abortion how to be forgiven.

Christians are citizens of both kingdoms. Spiritually, they are justified by faith apart from works of the Law. But insofar as they still live in the flesh, they must struggle against sin, both their own and the sin that plagues the world and that harms their neighbors. The Law continues to accuse them and bring them to the Gospel (the theological use of the Law). It also serves as a guide to help them live a life that is pleasing to God (the didactic use of the Law).

But most important to the temporal kingdom is the first use of the Law, the civil use, which acts as a curb to external sin. The civil use of the moral law, like the laws of the state, aims at external compliance. It cannot change anyone on the inside or make anyone righteous before God. But without external moral constraints on our behavior—as provided by civil government, cultural norms, the threat of punishment, and reinforced by guilt, shame, and a desire to please others—sinful human beings could never come together into a society.

So Christians are right to apply moral standards to the secular sphere. They should work for justice and promote the common good. This includes restraining evil by means of civil laws and good government. Christians can apply moral truth to criticize their leaders, their institutions, and their cultures.

Because God's temporal kingdom is governed by His Law, ideologies and practices that deny the reality of the moral law—such as moral relativism, utilitarianism, permissiveness, and the notion that morality is nothing more than a social or personal construction—are not in accord with the doctrine of the two kingdoms.

THE TEMPORAL KINGDOM AND THE CREATION

God also governs His temporal kingdom by virtue of His creation. Another misconception about the doctrine of the two kingdoms is that the kingdom of the left hand is merely about human government. It includes that, to be sure, but it also has to do with God's creation and His sustaining of the entire universe. The so-called laws of nature—by which physical reality functions in a consistent and predictable way—come from God, who built them into His creation. These laws, discovered by science and followed by engineers—

making it possible to build airplanes and satellites and computers—constitute not just created objects but a created order.

But God's involvement in His creation goes beyond the mechanistic repetition of natural laws. His power is such that He providentially cares for His creation, both as a whole and in intimate detail. Not a sparrow falls to the ground, says Jesus, "apart from your Father" (Matthew 10:29). He "clothes" the lilies, part of the transient "grass of the field," with their beauty (6:30). The scope of God's continual creation and His providence is celebrated in Psalm 104, which says of young lions, storks, rock badgers, the teeming creatures of the sea, and all of His "creatures,"

These all look to You,
    to give them their food in due season.
When You give it to them, they gather it up;
    when You open Your hand, they are filled with good
    things.
When You hide Your face, they are dismayed;
    when You take away their breath, they die
    and return to their dust.
When You send forth Your Spirit, they are created,
    and You renew the face of the ground. (vv. 27–30)

Even animals "look to" God to provide their needs. They take joy in His presence and are "dismayed" when they cannot perceive Him. The point is, the doctrine of the two kingdoms involves a specific theology of creation.

Ideologies and worldviews with a different understanding of physical reality are not in accord with the doctrine of the two kingdoms. Clearly, those who do not believe in God's creation do not believe in the doctrine of the two kingdoms. This goes beyond, though it arguably includes, adherence to creationism, the insistence that the creation account in Genesis is historical. The "createdness" of the universe has other implications. For example, contrary to the beliefs of Hinduism and Buddhism, which teach that the physical realm is an illusion, the universe does exist. Physical reality, however, is not *all* that exists, contrary to what the naturalists and materialists say. Nor are the physical universe or natural forces to be identified as God or as gods, as in pantheism and animistic religions, respectively.

To believe that the universe is created is also to recognize its order and design. Thus it can be known by reason. The universe shows signs of its origin in the mind of God, so it can be known by other minds. This is contrary to irrationalism and subjectivism, the post-modernist notions that objective truth does not exist or is unknowable. This is also contrary to the existentialist contention that the objective universe is meaningless.

Darwinism denies the Genesis account of creation and thus undermines the authority of Scripture. One can argue that nature must be understood by reason alone, without reference to the Word of God, which is the way we know the spiritual kingdom. Scientists, therefore, must follow their own rational methodology apart from any kind of divine revelation as they form conclusions about the natural order. It must be remembered, however, that the two kingdoms, while distinct, are connected to each other. The heavenly kingdom, as revealed in God's Word, rests on certain historical, objective, physical facts in the earthly kingdom—such as the incarnation of the Son of God, His atoning death on the cross, and His resurrection. These saving events are revealed in the Word of God, but they are nevertheless actual events. They are miraculous and so could not be deduced by reason alone, and yet they happened in the world. The same can be said of the creation. Science could not be expected to uncover its details, which elude empirical observation and can only be known through the Word, but if the doctrine of creation is true, it must have actually happened.

The other problem of Darwinism and its incompatibility with "createdness" as taught by the doctrine of the two kingdoms is its insistence that evolution is a function of random mutations: the human species came about *randomly*, as a result of innumerable chance mutations that proved to have survival value. According to Darwinists, this sequence of accidental happenings, filtered by natural selection, accounts for how human beings achieved consciousness, rationality, and civilization. Some Christians try to reconcile the role of God as creator with evolution, claiming that God created life *by means of* the naturalistic processes that Darwin described. But Darwinism insists that evolution is "nondirected." The very point of natural selection is its randomness. Theistic evolution agrees no more with Darwinism than creationism does.

Perhaps the most pressing opposition to the doctrine of creation today comes not from scientists—who, to their credit, agree with Christians on the objective existence and order of physical reality—but from postmodernists. Those who follow this strain of contemporary thought believe that reality is not a creation but a construction, that truth claims, moral systems, and social values are nothing more than cultural constructs and impositions of political power. According to this view, truth and morality are relative. Objective truth claims and moral absolutes are also always to be held in suspicion because they are acts of oppression. The only means of liberation is for individuals and marginalized groups to deconstruct the ideas of the *status quo* and to construct their own alternative truths and moral imperatives. Under postmodernists, God is no longer recognized as the source of truth and the source of the Law. Rather, human beings are their own creators and their own lawgivers, taking the place of God.

The Lutheran doctrine of the two kingdoms gives a basis for reason and rationality, without succumbing to the reductionism of the Age of Reason and the materialistic rationalism of modernism. The two kingdoms' teachings about creation give a basis for science, objectivity, and natural law, countering postmodernism, while still giving a place for mystery.

THE TEMPORAL KINGDOM AND VOCATION

God works in His temporal kingdom by means of vocation; that is, by working through human beings in the ordinary tasks and relationships of earthly life.

That Christians have a double life, as citizens in both of God's kingdoms, is a continual theme in Luther's writings. Christians are simultaneously saints and sinners. Spiritually, they are clothed in Christ's righteousness. And yet, they still live in the flesh, where they must struggle against sin and perform good works. This paradox leads to another: "A Christian is the most free lord of all, and subject to none; a Christian is the most dutiful servant of all, and subject to every one" (LW 31:344). By virtue of Baptism and having been justified by grace through faith in Jesus Christ, a Christian is free from sin, death, and the Law. Whereupon, God sends the Christian into the world to live out this faith in service to everyone; that is, to the Christian's neighbors. This happens in vocation.

The purpose of every vocation, as we discussed in the previous chapter, is to love and serve the neighbors that each vocation brings into our lives. Thus, in marriage we are to love and serve our spouse. In parenthood, we are to love and serve our children. In our jobs, we are to love and serve our customers. In our citizenship, we are to love and serve our fellow citizens. In the Church, we are to love and serve the other members of our congregations. In loving and serving our neighbors, God works through our vocations to bestow His blessings—our daily bread, the joys of family, peace, and security, the Word and Sacraments.

As we have seen, God's will for human society is for everyone, in each estate, to love and serve one another. But sin, as always, violates God's will. The doctrine of vocation can also serve as a critical model, a way to see why responsibilities and relationships are going wrong.

Instead of serving in our vocations, we want to be served. Instead of loving our neighbors, we often harm them or use them for our benefit. Parents are to love and serve their children, not abuse them or abort them. Husbands are to love and serve their wives, not belittle or mistreat them. Businesses should serve their customers, not cheat them. Government officials should love and serve those under their authority, not tyrannize and exploit them. In a church, members should love and serve one another, not stir up conflict by insisting on their own way.

And in general, ideologies and practices that reject marriage, that undermine parenthood, that reduce economic activity to selfish greed, that repudiate all civil government, and that have no use for the church as an institution are not in accord with the doctrine of the two kingdoms.

HIDDENNESS AS A MODE OF GOD'S PRESENCE

According to Luther's theology of the two kingdoms, God is hidden in His temporal kingdom. He is revealed in His spiritual kingdom. But hiding is a mode of presence. A little boy hiding in the house is *present*; he is just not seen. To be hidden means to be present without being perceived.

To say that God is hidden in the world means that He is *there*, that He is *here*, but we cannot see or otherwise detect Him. Incontrovertible scientifically-valid evidence to prove the existence of God and the truths of Christianity—what the New Atheists keep demanding—must always prove elusive. We have a God who hides Himself (Isaiah 45:15). Luther writes about how God hides Himself in the Sacraments, how in His wrath He hides His love, how His glory is hidden in the cross, how human vocations are His masks through which He works.

And yet God does reveal Himself to us. He does so by means of His Word, in which He is revealed and by which He builds His spiritual kingdom. God's Word reveals His incarnation in Jesus Christ. It tells us of His cross, in which He bore the sins of the world, and proclaims His resurrection. Furthermore, as Luther emphasizes, God's Word is not just a record of historical and theological information. It is God's instrument, through which the Holy Spirit convicts us of sin and creates faith in our hearts. God the Holy Spirit is thus truly present in His Word.

Sinners are made Christians by means of the Word and the Sacraments. By Baptism and their consequent faith in Christ, they become citizens of God's eternal kingdom. And yet, until they die and enter fully into the never-ending life that God has prepared for them, they remain citizens of God's temporal kingdom as well. Here they live out their faith—struggling with sin, bearing their crosses, growing in faith and holiness—in their God-given vocations. They are spiritually helped and sustained by their participation in the church, where they are continually fed by the Word and Christ's body and blood, receiving the forgiveness of sins and Christ Himself again and again. The Church—dwelling in both the spiritual and temporal kingdoms—recognizes that God's people have dual citizenship in both heaven and earth.

The spiritual Church consists of all believers throughout time. This spiritual Church is not limited to brick-and-mortar buildings, church membership rolls, or the local congregation. Rather, the one holy Church (*una sancta*) is the congregation of saints:

> If we will define the Church only as an outward political
> order of the good and wicked, people will not under-
> stand that Christ's kingdom is righteousness of heart
> and the gift of the Holy Spirit [Romans 14:17]. People
> will conclude that the Church is only the outward
> observance of certain forms of worship and rites.[4]

The Church, however, does not exist apart from the ordinary
physical mundane-seeming congregation. The spiritual Church
dwells in, with, and under the very physical church. That is to say, the
spiritual Church is present within the physical church. The physical
church may appear to be nothing more than a humble structure with
outdated sanctuary carpeting. The people in the congregation may
consist of blue-haired old ladies and burping babies. Nevertheless,
the Church is still something special, where Christ is hidden:

> The Church is not only the fellowship of outward
> objects and rites, as other governments, but at its core,
> it is a fellowship of faith and of the Holy Spirit in hearts.
> Yet this fellowship has outward marks so that it can
> be recognized. These marks are the pure doctrine of
> the Gospel and the administration of the Sacraments
> in accordance with the Gospel of Christ. This Church
> alone is called Christ's body, which Christ renews, sanc-
> tifies, and governs by His Spirit.[5]

The Church is part of the spiritual kingdom, ruled and governed by God's Word. But the Church exists in the world and thus
is also subject to kingdom-of-the-left-hand concerns. A Reformed

---

4   Apology of the Augsburg Confession, Article VII and VIII (IV), paragraph 13.
5   Apology of the Augsburg Confession, Article VII and VIII (IV), paragraph 5.

version of the doctrine of the two kingdoms teaches that the spiritual kingdom *is* the local church.[6] And the earthly kingdom consists of unbelievers, though Christians must live out their faith in this hostile environment. But the Lutheran view teaches that *both* kingdoms are good, being two different domains of the same King. The Church, like the Christian, inhabits both kingdoms. Congregations are subject not only to the laws of the state—zoning regulations, safety requirements, tax codes—but also to the moral law, which teaches how its members get along with one another. And yet, the spiritual kingdom—which spans all centuries, including all the saints in heaven—is present, though hidden, in a mundane local congregation where the Gospel is preached and the Sacraments duly administered.

The Christian's dual citizenship is experienced in vocation: individuals are spiritually helped and sustained by participation in their church, then God sends them back into their vocations, back into His temporal kingdom. Here God is hidden, and here the Christian is hidden as well. There may seem to be little difference between the Christian and the non-Christian in the work that they do, in their good or bad fortune, and in their outward appearance. But Christians have faith. They can see with the eyes of faith. "Set your minds on things that are above, not on things that are on earth," says St. Paul. "For you have died, and your life is hidden with Christ in God" (Colossians 3:2–3). Christians live on earth, *Christians live on earth, but their minds are set on what is above.*

6   See David VanDrunen, *Living in God's Two Kingdoms: A Biblical Vision for Christianity and Culture* (Wheaton, IL: Crossway, 2010). For the differences between this Reformed version of the two kingdoms and the Lutheran teaching see Jordan Cooper, "Lutheran Two Kingdom Theology Is Not Escondido Theology," *Just and Sinner* (blog), June 3, 2014, www.patheos.com/blogs/justandsinner/lutheran-two-kingdom-theology-is-not-escondido-theology and "A Critique of Escondido Two Kingdom Theology," *Just and Sinner* (blog), November 1, 2016, www.patheos.com/blogs/justandsinner/a-critique-of-escondido-two-kingdom-theology.

but their minds are set on what is above. Their participation in the spiritual kingdom gives them a different perspective on the temporal kingdom. Knowing God through His Word, they know by faith that He is also present and active in the world and in their temporal lives. God may be hidden, but Christians know by faith that He is present. Thus, they can give thanks for everything in their lives and do everything, no matter how mundane, in the name of Jesus. "And whatever you do, in word or deed, do everything in the name of the Lord Jesus," continues St. Paul, "giving thanks to God the Father through Him" (v. 17). The passage from Colossians concludes with exhortations about how Christians are to live out their vocations in the world, as wives and husbands, children and parents, employees and employers (3:18–4:1).

THE MASKS OF GOD

Lutherans have a theology of *presence*. God comes to us creatures of flesh and blood by assuming flesh and blood. He builds His spiritual kingdom by means of what is physical, so that the "incarnate and human God" comes to us by His Word (sound waves in the air; ink imprinted on paper) and Sacraments (the water of Holy Baptism, and the bread and wine of Holy Communion).

Martin Luther did not always recognize the ways in which God builds His spiritual kingdom by means of what is physical. Luther spent a period of his life living in extreme asceticism as a monk. He lived this way in an attempt to be more spiritual and less worldly. However, discovering the Gospel led Luther to embrace God's creation as good and even spiritually important. He then understood the spiritual as being constituted in the physical. Luther came to recognize the physical world as the means by which God is present in creation.

The interplay between the spiritual and physical is further articulated by Luther when he speaks of the "masks of God." Anthony Steinbronn sees this concept as foundational to all of Lutheran theology. Because of our sinful condition and God's grace, He comes to us through *means*:

> As a result of humankind's sinful nature human beings cannot see God, in His naked transcendence, and survive. Therefore since the fall of humankind into sin through the rebellion of Adam and Eve against God's will, there can be no unmediated relationship between God and humankind. God must wear a MASK in all of His dealings with human beings.[7]

To save us from our sin, God became incarnate in Jesus Christ, who has become our mediator, and He reveals Himself supremely in His cross, where His glory was hidden in His suffering. Says Steinbronn,

> A true and proper knowledge of God is derived solely in a theology of the cross. In His Son alone, who reveals the Father's heart and will, do we see and know God correctly. This knowledge of God is revealed to us through those MASKS ordained of God: (1) the Word of God; (2) His incarnation; (3) Baptism; and (4) the Lord's Supper.[8]

Just as God works through masks in His spiritual kingdom, says Steinbronn, He works through masks in His physical kingdom.

> Luther, in his explanation as to why God limits Himself through external means, speaks of HIS ORDERED POWER. God could save and work without externals

---

7   Anthony Steinbronn, *The Masks of God: The Significance of Larvae Dei in Luther's Theology* (Fort Wayne, IN: Concordia Theological Seminary, 1995), 4–5. Available online at www.reverendluther.org/pdfs2/The-Masks-of-God-Rev.Dr.Steinbronn.pdf.

8   Steinbronn, *The Masks of God*, 1.

and order, but it is His will to limit His power as He works among us. He does this so that, as He works through His created orders of church, home and government, His creatures have opportunity to share in His work. In these three orders, God seeks to govern His world for humankind's good and to reveal, in a daily fashion, His care toward all of humankind.[9]

CONCLUSION

So the doctrine of the two kingdoms cannot be used as an excuse for churches to either protect the *status quo* or uncritically follow cultural trends. Neither separatism nor dualism, the paradigm is rather a way of bringing together two different realms, while respecting the nature of each. Thus Christians can be both spiritual and secular. They can participate fully in the world without being worldly. The doctrine of the two kingdoms shows Christians how to live "in" the world without being "of" the world, as Christ prayed for them in His High Priestly Prayer (John 17:15–16).

---

9   Steinbronn, *The Masks of God*, 10.

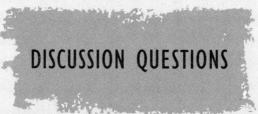

DISCUSSION QUESTIONS

1. What are some different ways that Christians today are confused about the relationship between the Church and the world? How does the doctrine of the two kingdoms help clarify the Christian's life in the world?

2. What are some misconceptions about the doctrine of the two kingdoms?

3. How is God actively present in the secular realm, even amid people who do not know Him?

CHAPTER 8

SANCTIFICATION AND THE CHRISTIAN LIFE

Instant is too slow in the world of the internet. Buffering downloads, lagging internet connections, and slow streaming are the source of many modern frustrations. If it takes more than five seconds, then there must be something wrong with the internet connection. If it takes more than ten seconds, then it is time to buy a new smartphone. The World Wide Web has provided a way to instantly search a cornucopia of information and download it to your smartphone; it has also made us inpatient, impetuous, and insisting that everything be instantly available to us.

Slow has become anachronistic in our instant culture. Nevertheless, there are some who still value the importance of slow and steady progress that requires patience and perseverance. A countercultural movement has formed amid this instant culture. This trend—known as the Slow Movement—has sought to reclaim a sense of slow in a world of fast. Slow food is a response to fast food. Slow living emphasizes simplicity and sustainability. The aim here is not more, more, more. Rather, it is focused on slow and steady progress.

Justification is instant. Sanctification is slow. The moment that the Holy Spirit leads a person to faith in Christ Jesus is the very moment of salvation. There is no buffering or prolonged download time when it comes to justification. It is the immediate and instant salvation that comes through faith in Christ Jesus. Sanctification, however, is far from instant. It is slow and steady progress toward a life of holiness. Sometimes, though, it is not all that steady; rather, it can be a steady conflict, full of ups and downs, failures and new beginnings. And it isn't always progress in the modernist sense of getting better and better, onward and upward, as if old people have become more holy than young people. It is, however, progress in the sense of a journey that is heading somewhere. Sanctification is the work of God, calling us to our vocations, providentially putting us through experiences that cause our faith and love to grow, and giving the Holy Spirit through Word and Sacrament. It is not immediate gratification or instant holiness. It is, however, the beautifully slow and eventful journey of the Christian life.

FREEDOM

One of the most fervent and deeply-held values for people today is the desire, the yearning, for freedom. Those who long for freedom the most, of course, are those who do not have it. Perhaps people today are not, in fact, as free as they long to be. Lutheran Christianity is characterized by freedom. Not in the sense of "do whatever you want"—since what we want will often destroy our own freedom and that of others—but in the sense of being liberated from spiritual bondage.

When Lutheran immigrants came to the United States from Germany, Scandinavia, and Eastern Europe, they sometimes received a chilly and perplexed reception from American Protestants. Sabbath-keeping was a major emphasis in nineteenth-century Protestantism, and here these Lutherans, after going to church on Sunday mornings, would go to beer gardens! They would listen to concerts! They would watch and play sports! And then on Christmas, they would decorate evergreen trees in their homes and even churches, like Druid tree worshipers! Are these people even Christians?

It soon became evident that these immigrants had an impressive vocation-inspired work ethic and a devout reliance on the Bible and the Gospel, but they seemed freer in their attitudes about recreation, aesthetics, and behaviors such as smoking and drinking than most American Protestants of their day. After all, Lutherans never had a Puritan tradition. They did have their Pietists, who sometimes rejected such worldly pursuits, but only as an individual discipline, rather than a social mandate. A major conflict between Lutheranism and American Protestantism came with the Prohibition Movement, with Lutherans and Catholics being perhaps the only religious groups to strenuously oppose the banning of alcohol.

Still today Lutherans tend to be quite different from the "handle not, taste not, touch not" (see Colossians 2:21) school of Christianity. They seldom belabor what kind of music they should listen to or whether they should patronize only "Christian" businesses. Their doctrines of vocation and the two kingdoms teach them that God is hidden in the world, just as He is revealed in the Church, so they see a Christian dimension even in the realms that are generally considered secular. More important, Lutherans believe that their relationship to God is based not on their works but in His grace; that is, in the forgiveness of their sins through Christ. Grace brings an end to endless self-scrutiny, parsing God's Law, and being obsessed with perfecting our own righteousness.

Now this does not mean that Lutherans are indifferent to the danger of sin and the importance of doing good works. The typical Lutheran is no worse and no better than the typical Christians of other confessions, and Lutheran churches have acquired a reputation for respectability. But, in light of the Gospel, good works can be performed in a spirit of freedom.

To be sure, some in the Lutheran tradition have been indifferent to sin and good works. But Luther and the orthodox theologians in his train have always battled these so-called antinomians (meaning those who are anti-Law). Today, when those who feel heavily burdened from a legalistic religion discover Lutheranism, their exhilaration and sense of freedom is so great that they sometimes veer toward antinomianism. There are also the so-called radical Lutherans, who downplay the third use of the Law (its use as a guide for Christians), insisting, among other things, that those transformed by the Gospel will automatically do what God requires of them. Yet, while there is some truth in that, it is not the whole truth.

Two of Martin Luther's greatest works are *The Bondage of the Will* (LW 33) and *The Freedom of a Christian* (LW 31). In the former, Luther argues against the great humanist Erasmus, insisting that human beings in our natural state have no free will at all because they are bound by sin. In the latter, Luther celebrates the freedom that Christians have through the Gospel. These two books sound contradictory, but they are not at all.

Our wills, Luther explains, are in bondage to sin. We cannot just "choose" to always do what is right. When we exercise our will to choose what we really, deep down want to do, our bondage is such that we will choose sin. Every. Single. Time.

Today, freedom is often associated with sin. And bondage is often associated with virtue. The "liberated" adolescent is a recurring motif in popular culture: A young man feels stifled by his family, his small-town community, his church, and all of their demands and expectations. But then he escapes. He goes off to the university or the big city. He is free! No more rules or restrictions! So he indulges in all the forbidden pleasures that he was never allowed to enjoy. Sexual freedom! Mind-expanding drugs! Liberation!

But Luther sees sin as enslaving and virtue as liberating. Luther bases this belief on the words of Jesus: "Truly, truly, I say to you, everyone who practices sin is a slave to sin" (John 8:34).[1] And people who have lived for a while know this is true. A porn addict is not free. An alcoholic or drug addict is not free. Nor are those who are in bondage to their other vices and bad habits—the egotistic reflexes that destroy relationships; the pride that keeps driving love away; the inclinations toward cruelty that keep ruining everything. The young man who enjoyed his freedom to break away from his home may find himself enslaved to his passions, to his peers, and to his most destructive appetites. And for all his self-disgust and strenuous willpower, he *cannot* change.

We have been freed from seeking to earn God's love so that we can love our neighbor, for his or her own sake.

But Jesus' next words show the power of the Gospel: "If the Son sets you free, you will be free indeed" (John 8:36). When we are justified not by our works but by faith in Christ, we are freed from the bondage of the will to sin. This means we are free, finally, to do what is right. We do what is right not because we *have to*—not as a way to earn salvation—but because we *want* to. We do good works for our neighbor not simply because we are supposed to and not to use the neighbor as a prop for our self-righteous display of our virtue; rather, we have been freed from

---

1   St. Paul explores this same idea in Romans 6. See also his exposition of Christian freedom in Galatians 5.

seeking to earn God's love so that we can love our neighbor, for his or her own sake. That is, we have been set free to care about our neighbor from the inside.

Often our moral actions are seen through our external behavior, though, as we say, our "hearts are not in it." Such external behavior can be a valuable moral discipline, but faith is a matter of the heart and faith changes our hearts. When we honestly face up to our own sinfulness and find our justification in Christ, how can we fixate on the neighbor's faults? Christ loves and died for the neighbor too, so if we are in Christ, how can we not partake of that love and that self-sacrifice?

Justification by faith allows us to do good works freely. The good works that we do in faith are more than just meaningless motions and empty endeavors. They are truly good works. Ethicists sometimes say that a moral action must be disinterested—detached from our own personal benefit or self-interests. If we volunteer at the homeless shelter because it makes a good photo op to help us get elected in a political campaign, that takes away much of the moral virtue. Serving others to serve yourself is not the same as genuinely caring about homeless people. Justification by faith means that we are not doing good works for ourselves. We have no need for good works to earn salvation. Since we are not "getting anything out of it," the good works that we do freely acquire genuine moral significance.

Of course, Christians do sin. We do not always love our neighbors or do good works spontaneously and freely. Part of us still lives in bondage. Although we have been redeemed, we are still "in the flesh" and still must struggle against our sinful nature. The Gospel does free us to do good works and to love our neighbor as we should. But we do not always do that. Or we do to a certain extent, but parts of our lives remain moral cesspools. Which means that Christians still need the Law, still need to be brought to repentance, and still need the Gospel.

This is the basis for the classic Lutheran paradox: a Christian is *simultaneously* a saint and a sinner. Clothed in Christ and His righteousness, a Christian is holy before God. And yet, the Christian is also a sinner, in constant need of Christ's forgiveness. It is not a binary sinner *or* saint; rather, it is both sinner *and* saint. A Christian has two identities, and the conflict between them shapes the Christian's spiritual life. This struggle between sin and grace—described also in Scripture as "the flesh" and "the Spirit" (Romans 8:1–17) and "the old self" versus the "new self" (Ephesians 4:22–24)—is that of sanctification.

> *A Christian has two identities, and the conflict between them shapes the Christian's spiritual life.*

This entails "mortification"—that is, putting to death—of the sinful nature. Philip Melanchthon, in the *Defense of the Augsburg Confession,* writes, "We teach this about the putting to death of the flesh and discipline of the body. . . . A true and not a false putting to death [mortification] happens through the cross and troubles, by which God exercises us."[2] The very troubles and hardships of life are means by which God sanctifies us! (More on this later.) "There is also a necessary, voluntary exercise," Melanchthon says. "This effort [at mortification] should be constant."[3] This latter point alludes to an important corollary: because Christ has set us free, we can now freely *cooperate* with the Holy Spirit in our sanctification.[4]

Since good works are the fruits of faith, the lack of them testifies to the need for a stronger faith. That comes, again, from the Gospel. A sinful Christian needs *more faith* in order to become free of that sin. This is why Christians need to go to church. In the Large Catechism,

---

2 Apology of the Augsburg Confession, Article XV (VIII), paragraph 45.

3 Apology of the Augsburg Confession, Article XV (VIII), paragraphs 46–47 .

4 See the Epitome of the Formula of Concord, Article II, paragraph 17 and the Solid Declaration of the Formula of Concord, Article II, paragraphs 65–66.

Luther explains that sanctification is the work of the Holy Spirit. And, as it says in the Third Article of the Apostles' Creed, the Holy Spirit works through the Church: "The Holy Spirit causes our sanctification by the following: the communion of saints or the Christian Church, the forgiveness of sins, the resurrection of the body, and the life everlasting."[5]

Our mortification—dying to sin and being made alive in Jesus— begins with our Baptism, in which we died with Christ and rose from the dead with Him (Romans 6:3–4). That Baptism, with its death and new life, is not just a onetime occurrence long ago but is operative "daily," says Luther, connecting it to the conflict of sanctification: "[Baptism] indicates that the Old Adam in us should by daily contrition and repentance be drowned and die with all sins and evil desires, and that a new man should daily emerge and arise to live before God in righteousness and purity forever."[6] Baptism also shapes the Rite of Confession and Absolution, involving contrition and repentance and the emergence of a new man who is righteous and pure. Baptism is also recalled in worship, which begins with the invocation of God's name ("In the name of the Father and of the Son and of the Holy Spirit"), the same name into which we are baptized. Worship also includes the recitation of the baptismal creed (the Apostles' Creed) and closes with blessings that recall those given at Baptism, such as the bestowal of "peace." The sermon, too, preaches Law and Gospel, creating repentance and faith. In Holy Communion, Christ bestows, with His body and blood, the forgiveness of sins.

Christians need all of this. The stakes of our sanctification are high. Although Lutherans strongly emphasize the assurance of salvation in the Gospel, they do not believe, as Calvinists and Baptists do,

---

5   Large Catechism, Part II, paragraph 37.

6   Small Catechism, The Sacrament of Holy Baptism.

that a Christian is "once saved, always saved." Persistent, unrepented sin, as well as neglect of the Means of Grace given in the church, can bring on the death of faith.[7] But when this happens, even the most hardened sinner can repent, receive Christ, and return to the redeemed status of the baptized.

And at the moment of our death, our flesh, our sinful human nature, will perish for good. All that will be left will be the new self, fully prepared for eternal life and ready for resurrection in the new creation. We will have been sanctified. And we will have become perfectly free.

FREEDOM → THE CHRISTIAN LIFE

In *The Freedom of a Christian*, Luther explains how freedom is at the heart of the Christian life, even as we are bound in love to our neighbors. The treatise begins with another paradox: "A Christian is a perfectly free lord of all, subject to none. A Christian is a perfectly dutiful servant of all, subject to all" (LW 31:344). Yes, we are free from sin and from the curse of the Law. But Luther also exults in freedom for its own sake: not only are all Christians priests, but they are also kings (an assertion all the more remarkable given the social and political conditions of his day). In this kingship of all believers, he says, "Every Christian is by faith so exalted above all things that, by virtue of a spiritual power, he is lord of all things without exception, so that nothing can do him any harm. As a matter of fact, all things are made subject to him and are compelled to serve him in obtaining salvation" (LW 31:354).

At the same time, the other side of the paradox also holds true: "Insofar as he is free he does no works, but insofar as he is a servant

---

7   See the Solid Declaration of the Formula of Concord, Article IV, paragraphs 31–33.

he does all kinds of works" (LW 31:358). Luther explains:

> A man is abundantly and sufficiently justified by faith inwardly, in his spirit, and so has all that he needs, except insofar as this faith and these riches must grow from day to day even to the future life; yet he remains in this mortal life on earth. In this life he must control his own body and have dealings with men. Here the works begin; here a man cannot enjoy leisure; here he must indeed take care to discipline his body by fastings, watchings, labors, and other reasonable discipline and to subject it to the Spirit so that it will obey and conform to the inner man and faith and not revolt against faith and hinder the inner man, as it is the nature of the body to do if it is not held in check. (LW 31:358–59)

Our "inner man" is free before God. But we must live in the world. We need to work for a living. We have relationships. And we must discipline ourselves. Our life in the world requires good works. That is to say, we have vocations.

And, as we have seen, the key to vocation and the key to good works is loving and serving our neighbors. "A man does not live for himself alone in this mortal body to work for it alone, but he lives also for all men on earth; rather, he lives only for others and not for himself," Luther writes. "To this end he brings his body into subjection that he may the more sincerely and freely serve others" (LW 31:364). Serving our neighbor entails self-discipline and acts of self-denial, but this service of others is to be done "freely." Both our relationship to God and our relationship to our neighbors, the realm of faith and the realm of good works, are characterized by freedom.

What Christ has done for the Christian, the Christian should do for the neighbor.

Luther goes on to describe what this service to the neighbor will look like: what Christ has done for the Christian, the Christian should do for the neighbor:

> Although the Christian is thus free from all works, he ought in this liberty to empty himself, take upon himself the form of a servant, be made in the likeness of men, be found in human form, and to serve, help, and in every way deal with his neighbor as he sees that God through Christ has dealt and still deals with him. This he should do freely, having regard for nothing but divine approval. He ought to think: . . . "I will therefore give myself as a Christ to my neighbor, just as Christ offered himself to me." . . . Just as our neighbor is in need and lacks that in which we abound, so we were in need before God and lacked his mercy. Hence, as our heavenly Father has in Christ freely come to our aid, we also ought freely to help our neighbor through our body and its works, and each one should become as it were a Christ to the other that we may be Christs to one another and Christ may be the same in all, that is, that we may be truly Christians. (LW 31:366–68)

At the end of *The Freedom of a Christian*, Luther draws together the polarities and paradoxes of the Christian life:

> We conclude, therefore, that a Christian lives not in himself, but in Christ and in his neighbor. Otherwise he is not a Christian. He lives in Christ through faith, in his neighbor through love. By faith he is caught up beyond himself into God. By love he descends beneath himself into his neighbor. Yet he always remains in God and in his love. (LW 31:371)

Here and throughout the treatise, Luther brings together the dualities of the Christian faith: the spiritual and the physical;

transcendence and incarnation; ascent and descent; faith and good works; love of God and love of neighbor. The Christian lives in all of these realms simultaneously, with the Gospel informing them both: "He always remains in God and in his love."

SANCTIFICATION IN VOCATION

As we have said, the Christian faith is lived out in vocation. Thus, sanctification primarily takes place in vocation. Luther's treatise *The Freedom of a Christian* is profoundly vocational, treating as it does the Christian's life in the world, love and service to the neighbor, and Christ's presence in vocation. So how does sanctification and its various aspects—mortification, good works, contrition, faith—play out in marriage, parenthood, the workplace, and our other callings?

When we love and serve our neighbors in our vocations, we are cooperating with God, who inhabits that vocation. This applies to the construction worker, who cooperates with the Creator in building a house; the pastor, who works with the Holy Spirit in proclaiming His Word; the husband, who emulates Christ's love of His Church in giving himself up for his wife; and so on.

Sometimes, though, we do not cooperate with God in our vocations. Instead of loving and serving the neighbors whom He brings to us in our various callings, we try to use our callings and those neighbors to serve ourselves. This may involve harming those neighbors, or despising or neglecting them, which puts us into conflict with God, meaning, we are sinning. Although God may still work through our vocations—getting the house built for the family that needs it through the sinful construction worker, conveying His Word and Sacraments by means of the sinful pastor, supporting the family through the sinful husband—sometimes, persistent neglect of God and neighbor can shatter the vocation. But more usually, these sins are momentary lapses that, nevertheless, must be dealt with by contrition and forgiveness.

Vocation is also an arena for mortification of the flesh. The construction worker may need to put in extra hours laboring to the point of exhaustion in order to get the house finished when the customer needs it. The pastor may have to work through, with faith, the hostility of certain members, frustration with his congregation's lack of growth, and spiritual assaults. The husband may need to battle sexual temptations and deny his own priorities for the sake of his wife. Recall what Melanchthon said, that the mortification that subjugates sin and forces us to turn to God happens "through the cross and troubles, by which God exercises us" and in the mortifications that Christians take on themselves as a "voluntary exercise."[8] In our various vocations, we can expect "troubles" outside our control. We can also expect that we will need to exercise self-discipline and take overt action in dealing with sin and temptation.

Troubles can be sanctifying because they often force us to pray. Catastrophic problems that we cannot deal with ourselves can lead us, out of a sense of desperation, to depend on God. The Australian Lutheran theologian John Kleinig says, "Strangely, we discover the mysterious power of God's Word, the hidden work of the Holy Spirit in and through the Word most clearly in temptation."[9] Drawing on Luther, Kleinig describes how temptations, trials, and even direct assaults of the devil can contribute to our sanctification:

> The devil's attack on us serves to strengthen our faith because it drives us back to God's Word as the only basis for spiritual life. We cannot rely on our own resources in the battle against Satan and the powers of darkness.

---

8   Apology of the Augsburg Confession, Article XV, paragraphs 45–46.

9   Kleinig, *Grace Upon Grace: Spirituality for Today* (St. Louis: Concordia, 2008), 21.

> If we rely on our own wisdom and power, we will fail. In that situation, our only hope is in Christ and His Word. Our spiritual weakness makes us trust in the power of the Holy Spirit and the wisdom of God's Word, which is "wisdom above all wisdom." Through temptation we learn to seek help from God in meditation and prayer. We walk with Christ on the way of the cross; we discover the spirituality of the cross. We do not experience the splendor of union with our heavenly Lord, but we share in His suffering and pain. We bear the cross together with our Lord as we suffer with Him. Through the attacks of the evil one we are drawn further out of ourselves and deeper into Christ.[10]

This is not the prosperity gospel or a theology of glory but the theology of the cross as it applies to vocation, sanctification, and the hardships of everyday life.

The doctrine of vocation is being rediscovered by many Christians today, but they often misunderstand it. Some recent treatments discuss vocation in terms of self-fulfillment. God's calling, they suggest, has to do with what gives you your greatest joy, or what makes you feel most alive. But what about jobs that are tedious and unfulfilling? Those are occupations, some are saying, not *callings*. They say that people stuck in dead-end jobs should look inside themselves to find out what they are truly passionate about as a way to discover what God is really calling them to do. On the other hand, some observers criticize the doctrine of vocation as applying only to the privileged.

To be sure, some of us are blessed with jobs that are fulfilling, that give us the opportunity to use our God-given talents in work that is satisfying and that gives us joy. Yet many others earn their living in

---

10   Kleinig, *Grace Upon Grace*, 22.

jobs that are boring and wearisome. Remember, though, that vocation is defined by its neighbors. Often the jobs that are unpleasant and lowly in the eyes of the world actually serve their neighbors in more direct ways than those that have a higher status. Trash collectors, hotel maids, and dishwashers surely bless their neighbors in more tangible ways than do professional athletes, derivative speculators, or movie stars. Yes, being a manual laborer is a calling, one that gives a God-given dignity and value to work that the world oftentimes sinfully scorns.

The point is, vocations are not necessarily for our personal fulfillment. Their primary purpose is for the neighbor, not for ourselves. They contribute to our sanctification through self-sacrifice, teaching us self-discipline, creating occasions for good works, and exercising our faith. Some vocations are mortifications in themselves. And yet, such is the grace and generosity of God that He gives us joy in our work, even under conditions that we would not expect to be joyful. There is the satisfaction for a job well done; the sense of accomplishment; enjoying the company of the people we work with. And even when our economic calling is unsatisfying, our other, more important vocations are designed to offer the richest fulfillment and joy: our marriage, parenting our children, the fellowship of our church, our involvement in our communities, our friendships and activities in the common order of Christian love.

> *Vocations are not necessarily for our personal fulfillment. Their primary purpose is for the neighbor, not for ourselves.*

Even those who are unfathomably blessed with economic callings that they delight in will find in their vocations struggles that contribute to their sanctification. This is true also of good marriages; happy parenting; and the best churches, communities, and friendships. Each of these, to one extent or another, will eventually bring trials,

AUTHENTIC CHRISTIANITY

maybe tribulations, and occasions to exercise our faith.

The contemporary Lutheran theologian Robert Benne suggests that *every vocation* has its particular temptations, struggles of conscience, and points of tension with the Christian faith. He describes his own calling as a Christian professor in a profession filled with anti-Christian biases. Similarly, he says,

> The Christian businessperson has to bring both intellectual and moral Christian resources to her work in business. She has to examine critically the moral quality of what is being produced and how it is being produced. She has to engage critically the assumptions that drive the business. The Christian social worker has to examine critically, from a Christian point of view, the various theories of human motivation and healing that currently inform the profession. The Christian lawyer has to assess critically the modern tendency to separate the law from morality and religion and to overcome that separation in his own practice of law.[11]

We could extend the principle to other kinds of vocation: Marriage requires faithfulness, which husbands and wives may be tempted to violate, whether from actual adultery or the soft adultery of pornography or "innocent" flirtations. Particular marriages, even strong ones, may have their own areas of difficulty—the differences in personality that can bring conflict—that couples have to work through. Similarly, parenting is full of challenges and individual heartaches. The best churches have their disputes and hurt feelings. Communities have their politics. Friendships have their spats and difficulties. Each of these points of trial in vocation becomes an occasion for struggle, self-denial, acts of love, and prayer. Also, in

---

11 Robert Benne, *Ordinary Saints: An Introduction to the Christian Life* (Minneapolis: Fortress Press, 2003), 172.

cases of failure, they become an occasion for repentance, confession, and absolution. As such, they contribute to the Christian's sanctification and spiritual growth. Notice that problems in vocation are not signs that the calling is invalid. Rather, they are to be expected. And they work, ultimately, for our good. Can we never leave a calling? If we have a job in which everything is going wrong, should we not look for a new one? If God has placed us in this miserable situation, that would seem to imply that we should just endure it, right? If we are supposed to stay in our callings, then we should still be working in those fast-food joints from our high school days.

Luther would sometimes exhort individuals to stay in their calling, for which his doctrine of vocation is criticized. Calvin, by contrast, urged people to better themselves whenever possible. But Luther was writing in the context of a static socioeconomic society, whereas Calvin was writing at a time of social mobility and the beginnings of a modern dynamic economy (both of which Luther's doctrine of vocation contributed to). When Luther said to stay in your calling, he was mainly making the point that you don't have to take monastic vows in order to be the best kind of Christian. But of course Luther knew that callings can change. That is, God can call a person to one vocation for a while and then to another. For example, Luther was once single. Then he was called to marriage. Then he was called to parenthood. His father started as a farmer, then became a miner, and then established a smelting business. He was initially a peasant and then rose to the ranks of the middle class.

Today we can expect to have numerous economic vocations in our lifetime. Often, our leaving a particular place of employment is due to situations outside our control. The factory shuts down. The company goes out of business. We get laid off. Unemployment is a trial and tribulation, but it can lead to a different calling. Often, other opportunities present themselves, and we might consider these opportunities to come from the hand of God.

Sometimes, the worker knows it is just time to leave. The atmosphere is toxic, the relationships are dysfunctional, and the work becomes emotionally and even spiritually draining. But aren't those problems occasions for sanctification, as we have just said? Yes. But, as Christians, we are free. Our status before God does not depend on our accomplishments at work. That frees us, so that we don't have to take our jobs quite so seriously.[12] We are free to stay, fighting the good fight. And we are free to leave. Running away from problems at work is not necessarily sinful; it is just not sanctifying.

Other kinds of vocations also change. A new economic calling may mean a calling to a new community and a new congregation. The decision to change one's calling can be agonizing and requires careful consideration and prayer. But we should not imagine that one decision represents God's will for our lives, as if the other would violate God's will; it is not as if there is a singular path that leads to God's blessing and all the other paths lead to divine neglect. God's calling comes through ordinary means—job offers, investment opportunities, consideration of our other vocations (such as our family's need for more money)—and we are to consider that wherever we end up is where God has placed us.

But there are some vocations that we must not run away from. Some vocations remain until death. The family vocations are permanent, though they change as time passes, ending only when death separates us. You will always be a father or mother to your children, even after they are grown. Marriage, too, is a permanent union in which a man and a woman become one organism, "one flesh" (Mark 10:7–9). But divorce is rampant in our time, including for Christians. It is of the greatest importance that husband and wife do not abandon each other when conflicts and trials come. Understanding

---

12 See Benne, *Ordinary Saints*, 169–71.

the doctrine of vocation can help couples overcome those problems, as husbands and wives learn to love and serve each other.

All of this may sound quite mundane, even nonspiritual. Surely God expects greater good deeds than what we do in the ordinary course of our jobs, our family life, and our other everyday vocations! For, as many believe, if our good works earn eternal life, they must be truly extraordinary—saving thousands of lives, saving thousands of souls, changing the world—in order to merit such an infinite payment. But, as St. Paul says, "We hold that one is justified by faith apart from works of the law" (Romans 3:28). *Good works are "apart" from our justification—not insignificant, just a separate category.* God calls us to faith, and then He calls us to distinct, unique spheres of service in the ordinary, physical, concrete world. In the course of that service, we "exercise" our faith so it grows stronger, and we grow in holiness.

> *Good works are "apart" from our justification—not insignificant, just a separate category.*

Some Christians are quite willing to be martyred for their faith, observes Einar Billing, but they cannot bear the minor annoyances of life:

> We often speak big words about [suffering], as if we yearned for martyrdom. Then God probably sets us in a position where we meet all kinds of small irritations and inconveniences. Immediately we begin to complain and fail altogether to realize that, although they are so insignificant, just these constitute the martyrdom God has sent to test our powers.[13]

There are ministers who are so caught up with "building the kingdom of God" that they neglect—or even mistreat, or sin against—their wives and children. God is not impressed with

---

13 Billing, *Our Calling*, 29.

grandiose accomplishments from someone who ignores his God-given calling to his wife and children.

Conversely, attending to the "small" and "insignificant" demands of our multiple vocations—at work, at home, at church, at the town square—can shape us in profound ways, teaching us how to love our spouse, our children, our customers, our fellow citizens, and our fellow Christians.

Ultimately, though, our sanctification is the work of God, who not only calls us to our vocations but also inhabits them, providentially putting us through experiences that cause our faith and love to grow, and giving the Holy Spirit through Word and Sacrament to make us holy.

Ours is a highly secularized world. The economy, governments, culture, and everyday life go on, with little reference to God. Lutheran Christianity teaches that God is hidden in the world in all of its secularity. That is to say, God is present, though unseen, in this secular realm, secretly caring for His whole creation. Furthermore, God sends His people, justified by faith, into that secular world to live out their faith and to serve others. Christians are free to participate in the secular-seeming institutions of family, the workplace, government, and culture, and these are precisely the domains where they find spiritual growth.

The secular, the ordinary, the mundane, the physical—these are not opposites of the "spiritual," as in many versions of Christianity. Rather, they are the texture of life, which is transfigured by God's presence, as discerned by faith. As John Kleinig explains it,

> By our practice of spirituality we are not raised to a higher plane above the normal, everyday, bodily life, but we receive the Holy Spirit from Christ so that we can live in God's presence each day of our lives as we deal with people and work, sin and abuse, inconvenience and

heartbreak, trouble and tragedy. We are not called to become more spiritual by disengaging from our earthly life, but simply to rely on Jesus as we do what is given for us to do, experience what is given for us to experience, and enjoy what is given for us to enjoy.[14]

14   Kleinig, *Grace Upon Grace*, 23.

DISCUSSION QUESTIONS

1. How is sin enslaving? How is the Gospel liberating? Explain Luther's paradox: "A Christian is a perfectly free lord of all, subject to none. A Christian is a perfectly dutiful servant of all, subject to all" (LW 31:344).

2. Sanctification has to do with how God makes us holy in the course of our lives and as we grow in faith. Does this mean that a seventy-year-old Christian is necessarily holier than a new convert or a newly baptized child?

3. How can the trials of life and struggles in our vocations help us grow in our faith and contribute to our sanctification?

CHAPTER 9

CONCLUSION

Signal-to-noise ratio compares the power of a signal to the power of background noise. The signal—meaningful information—must be stronger than the background noise in order to be heard. Background noise—unwanted signals—constantly interferes with the delivery and reception of meaningful information. Taking a phone call at the airport, having a conversation at a busy coffee shop, or hearing over young children fighting in the car are all examples of a signal-to-noise ratio that simply does not work. There are two ways around this problem: decrease the background noise or increase the power of the signal.

There is a staggering amount of background noise in our world today. This "background noise" goes far beyond the actual sounds emanating from our speakers and smartphones. Along with the many physical soundwaves traveling through the air, there is a tremendous amount of societal "background noise" traveling through our culture and into our minds: Modernity heralds unchecked progress, steady improvement, and the eventual perfection of society. Postmodernity clanks and clatters as it seeks to deconstruct modernity. Rather than the noisy gong of unchecked progress, postmodernity fills the world with the clanging cymbals of relativism, cultural constructs, and subjective truth claims. Like a noisy gong and clanging cymbals, modernity and postmodernity increasingly fill our world with distracting decibels. And there is yet other ambient noise: political squabbling, gaudy popular culture, economic uncertainty, and the nervousness of global terrorism.

Churches today are struggling to hear and to be heard over all these background sounds. There is a great deal of confusion in churches today as to what is noise and what is the signal. Should churches espouse a message of encouragement to discouraged people? Should churches join postmodern secularists and wallow in the dust of deconstructed truths? Are churches supposed to be places where the music is good, the coffee is strong, and the message is satisfying? Or are churches supposed to be places where authoritarian dogma is rejected as a relic from the past, every truth claim is equally accepted, and the message is intellectually stimulating? Rather than speaking over the noise, some churches are largely contributing to it and adding to the rising decibels of confusion. And, as a result, many churches are languishing. The signal—the Gospel of Christ Jesus—is going unheard while the noisy gongs and clanging cymbals of this world swell to a deafening crescendo.

Recovering authentic Christian spirituality does not require producing a new message. Nor does it mean joining the cacophony of our culture. Instead, recovering authentic Christianity requires increasing the clarity and power of the signal so it can be heard over the background noise.

LUTHERAN CHURCHES

We have been discussing Lutheran"ism," the Lutheran "tradition," Lutheran "theology," and Lutheran "spirituality." But we need to say more about Lutheran churches. Lutheran Christianity is not a separable religious ideology that can be carried from one nondenominational fellowship to another. Lutheran beliefs have to be embodied in specific congregations. Yes, a Lutheran perspective can be found, to a certain extent, among Christians who do not belong to a Lutheran church. But full-blooded Lutheranism has to be practiced in local communities of faith consisting of Christians who agree with one another theologically. Lutheran theology is always confessional and, in order for this to happen, there must be a shared confession. Moreover, Lutherans worship in a certain way. And worship—where the Word of God is proclaimed and the Sacraments are administered—is the living, beating heart of Lutheran spirituality.

Accurate numbers are impossible to come by, but there are reportedly 70–90 million Lutherans in the world. This makes it the third largest Protestant tradition in the world after Pentecostalism and Anglicanism.[1] But Lutheran church bodies, like those of other theological traditions, come in liberal and conservative varieties. There are also Lutheran state churches in the Scandinavian countries and Germany. Those northern European nations have become highly secularized. Church attendance is miniscule, though church membership remains high.

Some people in those countries go so far as to credit Lutheranism for their secularism! A Danish article on the impact of Lutheranism on the national psychology has the unintentionally humorous title

---

1   See Pew Research Center, "Global Christianity: A Report on the Size and Distribution of the World's Christian Population, December 2011," *Pew Research Center on Religion and Public Life*, http://www.pewforum.org/files/2011/12/Christianity-fullreport-web.pdf.

"Protestantism Has Left Us Utterly Confused." Its author, journalist Niels Ebdrup, flatly observes that "Lutheran Protestants are free from religiosity." He goes on to quote Matias Møl Dalsgaard, author of the Danish dissertation *The Protestant Self*:

> For centuries, Lutheran Protestant Christianity in Northern Europe and the US taught our ancestors that there was nothing they could do to make God think better of them. Neither good deeds nor giving money to the church was seen as having importance in the eyes of God.
>
> "For Protestants, life can be good just as it is. Life does not have to be lived in any particular 'religious' way in order to have a good relationship with God," says Dalsgaard.
>
> Protestants are free from obligations to God. They don't have to live according to strict rules. Instead they have been charged with a rather nebulous task.
>
> "Protestants are commanded to live an ordinary life together with other people. . . . You should actively be the one you are, where you are—and not think so much about who you are. This is a task given to us by God," says Dalsgaard.[2]

As we have seen, the doctrine of vocation and the doctrine of the two kingdoms *do* affirm the secular sphere in a way few other religions do. Traces of those doctrines are evident here. Also we can see the Lutheran reaction against Pietism ("Lutheran Protestants are free from religiosity") and the exaltation of the "ordinary" and vocation as living "an ordinary life together with other people."

---

2   Niels Ebdrup, "Protestantism Has Left Us Utterly Confused," *Science Nordic*, March 18, 2012, http://sciencenordic.com/protestantism-has-left-us-utterly-confused.

And yet, there is an antinomian flavor to these observations, as if our behavior makes no difference to God. More broadly, it is as if these authors affirm God's kingdom of the left hand, while ignoring God's kingdom of the right hand. Christ, the Gospel, the Word, the Sacraments—these do not rate a mention. It is obviously a misunderstanding of monumental and comical proportions to affirm the temporal kingdom while allowing the more important and all-defining spiritual kingdom to wither away! And yet we can see how deeply engrained Lutheranism is in the culture, even as the Church declines.

Today, the real center of Lutheranism is not in its European lands of origin but in Africa and Asia. There are some 35 million Lutherans in Europe—largely those on the books of the state churches—but there are more than 20 million in Africa and more than 10 million in Asia.[3] The fastest growing Lutheran Church is in India. Perhaps Africans and Asians have an awareness of the supernatural that is unencumbered by modernism and thus an appreciation for Lutheran sacramentalism that the West has lost.

As an illustration, there are some seven million Lutherans in the United States—about four million in the mainline Evangelical Lutheran Church of America (ELCA) and about three million in The Lutheran Church—Missouri Synod (our church body!) and smaller denominations, such as the Wisconsin Evangelical Lutheran Synod (WELS) and the Evangelical Lutheran Synod (ELS). But there are as many Lutherans in Indonesia as there are in the United States. Also as many in Ethiopia. And Tanzania.

So, Lutheran churches are "catholic" in the sense of being

---

3   The Lutheran World Federation, "The Lutheran World Federation 2013 Membership Figures," https://www.lutheranworld.org/sites/default/files/LWI-Statistics-2013-EN.pdf. The LWF is the largest association of Lutheran churches, but it does not include the conservative Lutheran churches, which can also be found around the world. These LWF statistics are useful, but they are far from complete.

worldwide and multicultural. What makes them "Lutheran" is their adherence to the Book of Concord (the *Concordia* in Latin)—the collection of ancient creeds, Reformation-era Confessions that defined the Lutherans over against both the Roman Catholics and other Protestant Movements, and the two catechisms used to teach the faith to this very day. Liberal Lutherans hold to the Book of Concord in a tentative way, as a historical document of their roots. Some state churches accept only certain portions of the Confessions. But "confessional Lutherans" believe it all—as a second authority to Scripture, for we believe the Lutheran Confessions are in accord with Scripture.

Notice that the authority for Lutherans is not Luther. He is our first and greatest theologian, but there are many others: the classical scholar Philip Melanchthon; the great systematizer and patristics scholar Martin Chemnitz; the various figures cited in this book, including Søren Kierkegaard, J. G. Hamann, C. F. W. Walther; and others. Yet of all theologians, Luther may be the most personal, the most pastoral, the most down-to-earth, and the one with the best sense of humor. In his writings and teachings, he is passionately committed to Christ and is a brilliant expositor of God's Word. Yet his polemical attacks on his enemies can be volcanic and obscene. His greatest crime is his tract *On the Jews and Their Lies* (1543), written during the mental decline of his last days. Never mind that in the early part of his career, in the formative years of his theology, he wrote *That Jesus Christ Was Born a Jew* (1523), denouncing the mistreatment of Jews and urging Christians to treat them kindly. But nothing excuses his later anti-Jewish ravings, and virtually all Lutheran denominations have repudiated them.[4] Luther always knew

---

4   See Uwe Siemon-Netto, *The Fabricated Luther: The Rise and Fall of the Shirer Myth* (St. Louis: Concordia, 1995).

himself as a wretched sinner, saved by the grace of God through Christ alone, and he would doubtless agree with his harshest critics about his faults. (The other hero of this book, J. G. Hamann, on the other hand, defended the Jews as the people of the Bible.)

In any event, it might seem inappropriate for a large and important Christian tradition to be named after one person. Indeed, the better term for Lutheran Christianity is *Evangelical*, just as those who followed the theology of Calvin can be called Calvinists but prefer to be called Reformed. In the days of the Reformation, Lutherans were called Evangelicals, underscoring that *everything* in Lutheran theology centered around the Gospel. But, even though Evangelical is still used in that sense in Europe, it has different connotations in English today, which often bring to mind evangelical politics or modern Evangelicalism.

Perhaps one of the best terms for this kind of Lutheran Christianity can be found in the name of the largest Lutheran church body in the world, the Ethiopian Evangelical Church Mekane Yesus (EECMY). *Mekane Yesus* means "place of Jesus." The name underscores the central Lutheran teaching that Christ is situated in the physical world, in the church, and that Jesus is truly present in the Word and Sacraments. As of 2016, the EECMY had over 8.3 million members, moving past the Church of Sweden as the largest Lutheran church in the world.[5] The EECMY is also breaking away from the more liberal churches in the Lutheran World Federation over sexual morality issues and is allying itself with confessional Lutheran bodies, such as The Lutheran Church—Missouri Synod.

Some Lutheran church bodies are ruled by bishops—with some claiming apostolic succession—while others are governed by elders

---

5   Matthew   Block,   "Ethiopian   Lutherans   Elect   New   President," *International Lutheran Council*, March 15, 2017, http://ilc-online.org/2017/03/15/ ethiopian-lutherans-elect-new-president.

or the congregation. But church government has to do with the earthly kingdom. What makes a local church "the place of Jesus" is the Word and Sacraments, the faithful preaching of God's Word and the faithful administration of Holy Baptism and Holy Communion. And for those you must come inside.

THE DIVINE SERVICE

If you walk into a traditional Lutheran church, you are leaving the contemporary world behind. The pastor is unlikely to be wearing skinny jeans and a hipster flannel shirt, as in congregations that strive to be contemporary. Instead, he will be wearing a white robe and colored vestments, like a priest out of the Middle Ages. The sanctuary will be centered not on a screen but on an altar. The choir will be out of sight. The room will be crowded with art—stained glass windows, statues, banners.

And when the service begins, the sense of being in another realm of being intensifies. Lutherans do not have to be absolutely uniform with one another when they worship, and some experiment with a variety of styles. But even the most "contemporary" tend to be litur-

The Divine Service . . . is called that not because in worship we are serving God, but because He is serving us.

gical—that is, formal, scripted, and going somewhere. The classic and definitive Lutheran form of worship is called the Divine Service. It is called that not because in worship we are serving God, but because He is serving us.

The Divine Service is the Catholic Mass, but with the prayers to the saints, allusions to our merits, and other biblically problematic portions left out. The Divine Service is the Mass pared down to Christ alone. The Divine Service begins with the Invocation—not a long prayer of the sort that begins board meetings, but a "calling

on" the triune God, naming the One we are worshipping and sum-
moning His presence: "In the name of the Father and of the Son and
of the Holy Spirit." Those are also the words of Baptism ("I baptize
you in the name of the Father and of the Son and of the Holy Spirit"),
so the words are accompanied by the sign of the cross, sketch-
ing a cross in the air or on one's heart, which is also a part of the
Baptism rite.

Then follows the Confession, in which the members of the congregation admit their sins. (You can do it individually to the pastor,
as in the Catholic Rite of Confession, but it can also be done col-
lectively, as in the liturgy.) Then comes the Absolution, when the
pastor forgives sins. Actually, Christ is forgiving their sins, but He
does it through the vocation of the pastor. (Remember how vocation
is about how God works through human beings?) Here the pastor
says, "Upon this your confession, I, by virtue of my office, *as a called*
and ordained servant of the Word, announce the grace of God unto
all of you, and in the stead and by the command of my Lord Jesus
Christ I forgive you all your sins in the name of the Father and of
the Son and of the Holy Spirit" (*LSB*, p. 185, emphasis added). Here
is more Baptism. Here is vocation. Here is God's Word. Here is the
Gospel of God's grace through Christ. The man in white at the front
of the sanctuary is making it all highly tangible.

Then comes the great liturgical set pieces that go back throughout
the history of the Church: The Introit, an opening Psalm. The Kyrie,
"Lord, Have Mercy." The Gloria in Excelsis, "Glory to God in the
Highest." These are typically chanted, not just by the pastor but particularly by the congregation. (Chanting is simply a way of singing
prose, with its irregular rhythm and varying sentence length.) Interspersed in the liturgy are prayers, including the historic "Collects"
prayed by the Church for centuries. The Creed. Bible readings from
the Old Testament, an Epistle, and a Gospel, selected according to

the schedule of readings known as the Lectionary. Also interspersed are Luther's innovations: hymns.

Lutheran worship is timeless. The structure of the Divine Service is ancient, dating back to the Early Church. The hymns, on the other hand, may have been written in the Middle Ages, the seventeenth century, the eighteenth, the nineteenth, the twentieth, the twenty-first centuries. The music of a typical service shows the constant interaction between the Church and the ages. It is important that not *just* the songs of our age be sung, but rather that the music of all times in the Church's history comes together as it is sung in this present moment.

All of this builds to the sermon, in which the pastor preaches on one of the Bible readings for the day, bringing out the Law and the Gospel, convicting his hearers of sin and convincing them of their forgiveness in Christ. Then the Offertory—not special music to go with the offering, but an ancient hymn built on Psalm 51, the prayer to "Create in me a clean heart, O God." Actually, *all* of the liturgical set pieces are based on Scripture. So the very texture of the liturgy is nothing less than the Word of God.

Then the Divine Service builds to its second climax: Holy Communion. More ancient liturgical songs: The Preface ("The Lord be with you"), the Sanctus ("Holy, holy, holy"), the Lord's Prayer ("Our Father who art in heaven"). Then the pastor says, or sometimes sings, the Words of Institution. And then the congregation greets Jesus, who is now among us, with the Agnus Dei ("O Christ, Thou Lamb of God, that takest away the sin of the world, have mercy upon us"). The congregation receives Christ's body and His blood, then sings the Nunc Dimittis ("Lord, now lettest Thou Thy servant depart in peace"). A Thanksgiving, another Collect, the Salutation and Benedicamus, and finally the Benediction, which sends us back into our vocations with a blessing.

Is it cool? At first it may seem so, since the Divine Service is so unutterably *different* from the easy informality that we are used to. But it soon becomes clear that our categories of time and fashion—what's cool and what's outdated, what's current and what's old-fashioned, what's the latest fad or belief system—mean nothing when you stand before the very presence of Christ. Our modern culture has lost a sense of the holy. That word on one level means "set apart," with holy things being kept distinct from what is "profane" or everyday. Many churches today expend great effort to make their services indistinguishable from "everyday life," but the pop music, new pastoral fashion, and concert-like atmosphere only succeed in making their worship services "profane." Lutheran worship, on the other hand, creates the awe, mystery, and beauty of holiness.

THE NEWNESS OF THE OLDNESS

We have been making strong claims for Lutheranism and for what happens in a Lutheran worship service. And yet, it can all seem very weak, very ordinary. Although it speaks clearly to the struggles of contemporary culture, it is often out of sync with popular trends and movements. The Lutheran Confession is far from a theological jellyfish that aimlessly shapes and shifts around the ever-changing culture. Rather than chasing after the newest "cool," Lutheran theology steadily proclaims the clear and consistent message of Law and Gospel, Word and Sacrament, and the beautiful hiddenness of God in what may appear to be just ordinary life.

If you go to an actual Lutheran church, after the newness—or perhaps oldness—of the liturgy wears off, it may seem very ordinary, very mundane. Most of the people in the congregation may be much older than you. There may also be crying babies distracting you from the worship. (Because Lutherans believe baptized babies are fully Christian and that the Holy Spirit works through the Word no matter the age, they are not big on nurseries. And they tend to resist exiling the young to "Children's Church," thereby teaching them not to attend regular worship services.) And sometimes the sanctuary gets too hot or too drafty. And your attention phases in and out. Do not worry; you are in the right place. God is hidden here.

God is hidden in the Word, the Sacraments, the vocation of the pastor and the parents with the crying babies. Not in glory, but in the cross, where Christ emptied Himself of His glory to meet us where we are. It is all so ordinary and mundane that you may overlook it if you are not careful. Do not overlook it. Revel and rejoice in the ways that God is both hidden and present in Word and Sacrament ministry of the local congregation.

THE NEXT FIVE HUNDRED YEARS

There is the growing sense that twenty-first century Christianity could use another Reformation. Five hundred years after the outbreak of the Protestant Reformation, contemporary churches seem adrift, confused, and dysfunctional. Many modern Christians have a lukewarm theology that has left them ill-equipped for the challenges of secularism, postmodernism, and cultural change. Many Christians add to the noise and confusion by arguing that churches need to make changes to reach the "unchurched." According to many so-called experts, if churches really want to engage people who are "spiritual but not religious," then we must resemble a coffee shop more than a church. *Churches are deluding themselves that they must dilute themselves.* It is clearly time for another Reformation.

We believe that the same theology that ignited the Reformation five hundred years ago could bring reformation to the church of the twenty-first century. We believe that Lutheran theology offers an articulation of Christianity that can resonate with postmodernists, secularists, and those who are "spiritual but not religious." We believe that this confession of faith is the authentic Christian spirituality that can engage both nonbelievers and burned-out believers. We believe that reversing the tide of "nones" (people who do not identify with any religious affiliation) requires a stronger—not weaker!—message.

If the future of North America is going to be different from the rampant secularism of Europe, then churches must recover and reclaim an authentic and robust Christianity. The future of Christianity does not depend on making minor stylistic changes. Instead of endlessly tinkering with style, the years ahead will require Christianity to deal with the content of its teaching. The church's next era should recover the authentic Christianity of the past and apply it fearlessly to whatever the future will bring. Christianity's continuing relevance can be made clear with the help of the distinctly Lutheran insights: the nearness of God, the justifying peace of the cross, the mysterious hiddenness and presence of God in the Sacraments, and the divine purpose found in vocation.

> *Instead of endlessly tinkering with style, the years ahead will require Christianity to deal with the content of its teaching.*

We have come five hundred years since the Reformation. Since then, the prominence, the influence, and the political power of the church have faded. But that clears the way for a purer, more faithful church. The time for the theology of glory is over. Now the church can embrace the theology of the cross.

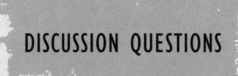

DISCUSSION QUESTIONS

1. Some congregations today are "nondenominational," allowing members to hold any number of different theologies. Could the beliefs described in this book—or perhaps some of them—be practiced in that context? Why does the Lutheran theology and spirituality described here call for involvement in a distinctly Lutheran church?

2. A Lutheran congregation in a Lutheran denomination seems little different from other institutional churches. It will have its own history, traditions, and cultural connections. It will have its own problems, inconsistencies, and personalities. Can God be "hidden" in such an institution? Why or why not?

3. How are the various teachings described in this book embodied in Lutheran worship?

4. How might Lutheran Christianity become a catalyst for a new Reformation?